Key to the Keystone State:
Pennsylvania

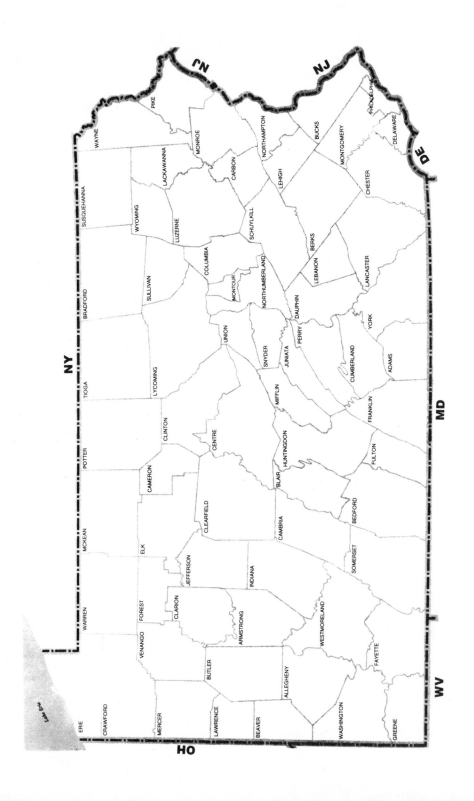

Key to the Keystone State
PENNSYLVANIA

Fourth Edition

League of Women Voters of Pennsylvania

THE PENNSYLVANIA STATE UNIVERSITY PRESS
University Park and London

Fourth Edition, published 1989

A project of the League of Women Voters Education Fund

Printed in the United States of America

For permission to reproduce any part of this book, write:

League of Women Voters of Pennsylvania
P.O. Box 607
Harrisburg, Pennsylvania 17108–0607

Library of Congress Cataloging-in-Publication Data:

Key to the Keystone State, Pennsylvania.

Includes index.
1. Pennsylvania—Politics and government—1951–
I. League of Women Voters of Pennsylvania.
JK3616.K48   1989   320.4748   87–43184
ISBN 0-271-00635-8

Contents

List of Charts and Illustrations

Foreword

The League of Women Voters is a nonpartisan political organization that encourages citizens to play an informed and active role in government. An outgrowth of the women's suffrage movement, the League was founded in 1920 to encourage women to exercise their newly-won franchise in an informed manner and to realize and develop the influence that the individual's vote can have in a democratic society. Today the League has both male and female members, but our basic goal is still the same: we believe that an informed citizen is a better citizen.

About twenty years ago the League of Women Voters of Pennsylvania realized that there was no easily readable, readily available book to explain to Pennsylvanians how their government operates. This volume, now in its fourth edition, fills that void. It is a textbook in colleges and high schools and a reference source in businesses, libraries, government offices, and homes throughout the state.

If you have unanswered questions about Pennsylvania government, consult your telephone directory for a local chapter of the League of Women Voters or call our Legislative Information Center toll-free: 1–800–692–7281.

We would like to express our appreciation to Senator Vincent J. Fumo for his assistance in securing a grant from the Commonwealth of Pennsylvania for this project. We would also like to thank the following

corporations who contributed their financial support to the publication
of this book:

Air Products and Chemicals, Inc.
ARA Services, Inc.
Pennsylvania Power & Light Company

Marilyn F. Brill, President
League of Women Voters of Pennsylvania

Nancy G. Smith, Project Director
Key to the Keystone State

Preface

Modern state government is complex and greatly affects the lives of all Pennsylvanians. Citizens need to understand where political decisions are made and how they can influence them. *Key to the Keystone State* responds to that need. It is a basic guidebook on the structure and operation of Pennsylvania government. No volume of this size could include everything about state government and so a section on further information is provided that lists additional sources.

Although the basic structure of Pennsylvania government has remained almost the same since 1790, changes have been made to respond to the demands of the times. In the last twenty-five years, for example, the equal rights and environmental rights amendments have been added to the constitution, the departments of aging, environmental resources, and community affairs have been added to the executive branch, and other departments have been consolidated or modernized.

In the text, the word "commonwealth," an old English term popular in colonial days, is used interchangeably with "state." Pennsylvania is one of four states that still use the term. Another name for Pennsylvania, the Keystone State, goes back almost as far. Pennsylvania was seen as the keystone that held together the arch formed by the original thirteen colonies.

The editors are indebted to the many state government officials and to the Board of Directors of the League of Women Voters of Pennsylvania who generously provided information and comments as the project progressed. We are also grateful to Edith Stevens, Mary Jane Turner, James J. Wetzler, and William H. Nast, who read the manuscript. We acknowledge the contribution of our associate at M C Consultants, Janet Schlesinger, for her thoughtful and perceptive criticism. We also recognize our debt to the editors of the previous editions of *Key.*

We have strived to ensure accuracy as of the date of publication, and we accept responsibility for what is in the book. If errors are found, please send corrections to the League of Women Voters of Pennsylvania, P. O. Box 607, Harrisburg, PA 17108–0607

Terese S. Piccoli   Susan E. Brandt
Editor   Technical Editor

1

The Pennsylvania Constitution

A constitution is the fundamental law legitimizing a state or nation, defining the limits as well as the obligations of government. A constitution typically includes a declaration of the rights of citizens, the definition of powers of government, and the means for amendment. State constitutions are subordinate to the United States Constitution.

The federal Constitution is brief and general and its inherent flexibility has enabled it to be adaptable for two centuries. State constitutions, by contrast, are usually far more detailed, requiring frequent amendments to meet the demands of changing times. When the need for change is too extensive to be met by amendments alone, a constitutional convention may be called.

Foundation of Pennsylvania Government

Four constitutional conventions have been called in Pennsylvania since the first state constitution was adopted.

Early Constitutions

The Constitution of 1776

The Second Continental Congress recommended in May 1776 the establishment of new state governments to supplant the existing colonial governments. Under Benjamin Franklin's leadership, Pennsylvania was the first to act on this resolution. Drafted in the midst of the struggle for American independence, the first constitution of Pennsylvania was adopted in Independence Hall, Philadelphia, in September of the same year.

The constitution provided for a single house legislature called the Assembly. All sessions of this body were to be public, with proceedings published weekly. The Assembly was to be apportioned every seven years on the basis of the number of taxable inhabitants. Some drafters, suspicious of power vested in a single leader, set up a twelve-man executive council. One member of this council was to be elected annually as president.

A court system was established with a Supreme Court on the state level; a Court of Common Pleas, Orphans' Court, and courts of session on the county level; and justices of the peace on the local level. Judges, appointed by the Executive Council with limited terms of seven years, were subject to removal by the Assembly. Provisions were also made for the election of sheriffs, coroners, registers of wills, and recorders of deeds at the county level.

A Council of Censors was created to evaluate Assembly members and to ensure that the provisions of the constitution would be carried out. This council was also empowered to call a convention to revise the constitution.

The Declaration of Rights of this constitution has been incorporated in all subsequent constitutions of Pennsylvania with few changes.

The Constitution of 1790

The weaknesses of the Constitution of 1776 became evident and major objections surfaced over the Executive Council, the single legislative body, and the Council of Censors. In 1789 the Assembly called a convention to rewrite the constitution.

Although many differences of opinion persisted among the state's radical and conservative leaders since the adoption of the first constitution, the two factions were able to compromise their differences at the convention. As a result, the second constitution contains important ideas from each viewpoint and was adopted with little dissension.

The new constitution provided for a strong governor, created a second legislative body, the Senate, and abolished the Council of Censors. The governor was given the power to recommend and to veto legislation, and to call special sessions of the legislature. The earlier executive council's appointive powers were transferred to the governor. The constitution also provided the basis for a public system of education.

Circuit courts were added to the previous judicial system, and judges were given life tenure, subject to removal by impeachment.

The Constitution of 1838

While the first two constitutional conventions had been held without benefit of public referendum, the question of calling a convention to revise the constitution was approved by the voters in the gubernatorial election of 1835.

The prevailing mood of the country favored more popular control of government in order to protect people from the abuse of power and to make office holders more responsive to the public will. Since a strong executive was increasingly distrusted, the convention curtailed the governor's power by increasing the number of local elective offices that had previously been appointive. Limitations were placed on the legislature's power to grant corporate and banking charters. The delegates also limited the governor's term and shortened the tenure for judges, who would, however, still be appointed.

Bitter arguments enlivened the convention. Efforts failed to eliminate the taxpaying requirement for voters and to extend suffrage to all males regardless of race, though both measures had strong support.

The document that emerged from the bitterly divided convention increased the popular voice in government, but it left the main structure of the previous constitution unchanged. It was approved by a narrow margin of the electorate.

Amendments to the 1838 Constitution

The Constitution of 1838 was amended four times, resulting in changes that are still in effect. In 1850 an amendment was passed to provide for popular election of judges. In 1857 the power of the legislature to create new counties was curbed, and the borrowing power of the state was limited. The composition of the House of Representatives was set at one hundred members elected in single-member districts. An amendment in 1864 provided for absentee voting for soldiers on military duty. The powers of the legislature were also reduced. Bills, except appropriation bills, were limited to one subject, and the title of each bill was to clearly state its purpose. In addition, the legislature was forbidden to act on matters that belonged to the courts. By amendment in 1871, the State Treasurer was elected by the people rather than by the General Assembly.

The Constitution of 1874

As a result of fraudulence and favoritism, disillusionment with politics and the legislative process was common throughout the country after the Civil War. The Constitution of 1874 was born out of the nationwide reform movement of the 1870s, when many state constitutions were rewritten.

The proliferation of local and special laws in Pennsylvania dealing with roads, bridges, elections, and schools caused confusion as regulations differed from one district to another. The governor referred to these laws and to the "patchwork character" of the constitution's cumbersome amendments when he asked the legislature to issue a call for a constitutional convention in 1871.

The convention, which began in 1872, dealt primarily with the reform of the legislature, the judiciary, and the election process; restraint of corporations, railroads, and municipal finances; and the abuse of the Assembly's power to grant charters and pass special legislation.

To address these issues, the convention made the following changes: (1) The House of Representatives was doubled to two hundred members and the Senate was set at fifty on the theory that more legislators would be more difficult to corrupt. (2) The size of a majority required to pass bills was increased from two-thirds of those present and voting to two-thirds of those elected. (3) The General Assembly was to meet biennially instead of annually. (4) To limit the power of the legislature, the convention prohibited special legislation to grant charters to private or municipal corporations. (5) Uniformity of taxation and exempting certain types of property from taxation further restricted the legislature's power.

While lessening the power of the legislature, the Constitution of 1874 enhanced the governor's powers. It added the item veto on appropriation bills to the chief executive's powers and the power to call special sessions. A two-thirds vote of the legislature would be required to override the governor's veto of a bill. This constitution provided that the governor could not serve more than two consecutive terms of four years and created the office of lieutenant governor. It also limited the governor's power to grant pardons.

In spite of lengthy convention argument, only modest changes were made in the judicial article. The method of choosing judges and the question of an intermediate court were sharply debated. In the end, no provision was made for an intermediate court, but the legislature could create one if necessary. Popular election of judges was retained, following much argument between those who preferred the appointment of all judges and those who desired the appointment of only Supreme Court judges. The debate continues to this day.

Provision by the Commonwealth for the education of all children over six was included in the document, strengthening the education article of the previous constitutions.

Great controversy over election reform followed the disclosure of irregularities in voting and registration in some areas of the state. Reform included requirements for numbering ballots, recording the numbers, and an option of signing the ballot so that the voter could be certain it was recorded accurately. Suffrage under the new constitution was extended to nonwhites to conform with the recently passed Fifteenth Amendment to the federal Constitution. Taxpaying qualifications for voters were retained, and the vote for women was considered and defeated.

Although forbidden by the enabling statute to change the Declaration of Rights, which the legislature declared should "remain forever inviolate," the convention actually strengthened those provisions. It extended greater freedom to the press, authorized the waiver of trial by jury, and increased the guarantee of free elections. The new constitution passed by an overwhelming majority.

The Constitution of 1874 was a lengthy document that embodied many earlier changes made by amendment to the third constitution. Although detailed, it was flexible enough to permit the creation of government agencies to meet new social and industrial demands. After its adoption, no amendments were added for a generation, and it remained in effect until 1968. Between 1901 and 1959, eighty-six amendments were placed before the voters. Most of the fifty-nine approved by them were minor, permitting exceptions to general provisions rather than affecting fundamental law. Major state reforms realized during this period were instituted by legislative statute rather than by amendment.

In the elections of 1966 and the primary election of 1967, the voters approved major amendments that drastically revised many sections of the constitution. Among these changes were the following: the General Assembly became a continuing body meeting annually, the denial of civil rights to any person was prohibited, the governor and lieutenant governor would be elected together and would be eligible for one successive term, a training course for new magistrates who were not lawyers would be required, and an emergency procedure for amending the constitution was established.

The task of modernizing the rest of the document was left to the Constitutional Convention of 1967–68.

The Constitution Today

The Constitution of 1968

The Constitutional Convention of 1967–68 was approved by the voters in May 1967. It was not authorized to draw up a new constitution but was limited to four subjects: administration of justice, state finance, local government, and legislative reapportionment. Besides the subject areas, other restrictions also applied. The convention convened on December 1, 1967, and was required to complete its work no later than February 29, 1968. The convention could not alter the "uniformity clause," which, according to a state Supreme Court ruling, prohibited a graduated income tax. It was also prohibited from altering the restriction that the motor fuel and license fees be used for anything other than highways and bridge construction and repairs.

The work of the convention resulted in five questions that were placed before the voters in April 1968. These referenda (1) specified the number of 203 representatives and created a legislative reapportionment commission; (2) provided for a limit on state borrowing based on tax revenue, ensured that a balanced budget and financial plan for the state would be prepared, and required that all departments would be subject to audit; (3) permitted certain tax exemptions for needy citizens, exempting certain classes of property from state and local taxation, including the property of public utilities; (4) provided for home rule for all units of local government, optional forms of government, uniform procedures for merger, consolidation and boundary change, intergovernmental cooperation and area governments, local finance and debt limits, and local apportionment; (5) established a unified judicial system under the Supreme Court, created a Commonwealth Court, and modernized the minor courts; provided for the qualifications, selection, tenure, removal, discipline, and retirement of justices, judges, and justices of the peace; and created the Judicial Inquiry and Review Board.

The approval of these proposals set in motion a three-year transition period. As part of this process, an amendment calling for merit selection of judges was placed before the voters in the May 1969 primary, but it failed to receive approval.

The combination of the amendments and the work of the limited Constitutional Convention of 1967–68 resulted in a document that is substantially revised and free of much legislative detail which had encumbered the Constitution of 1874. By proclamation of the governor the revised document is known as the Constitution of 1968.

Additional amendments have been added to the constitution since the 1968 convention. Most notable are the equal rights amendment, and the environmental rights amendment, acknowledging the people's right to clean air and water and preservation of the environment. Both were passed in 1971.

Amending the Constitution

Article XI outlines the procedures for amending the constitution. An amendment must be passed by a majority vote of the members elected to each house of the legislature in two successive sessions of the General Assembly and then be approved by a majority of the electorate. An amendment may originate in either the House of Representatives or the Senate. The same amendment may not be submitted to the voters more than once in five years. If two or more amendments are placed on the ballot, they must be voted upon separately.

An emergency method of amending the constitution is included in Article XI. It requires a two-thirds majority vote of the members elected to each house, and final approval of the amendment is by a majority of the electorate voting at least one month after the action of the General Assembly.

The emergency procedure has been used three times—in 1972, 1975, and 1977. In each case, the voters approved a referendum authorizing the use of state funds for relief to areas that had been hit by storms or floods. The latest, approved in 1977, appropriated money for disaster relief in the future.

Calling a Constitutional Convention

While specific procedures for amending the constitution are included in the document, those for calling a constitutional convention are not. Such procedures may be devised by the legislature at the time a call is issued. The five constitutional conventions in Pennsylvania have been called in varying ways. Neither of the first two conventions was called by a vote of the people, nor were those constitutions submitted to the public for ratification.

The 1837 convention call required a referendum, as did the subsequent calls. In 1871 the General Assembly only presented the question of calling a constitutional convention, writing the enabling legislation after the call was approved. The 1967 legislature included the procedures in the convention call and stipulated that the election of delegates would take place at the next election.

The Pennsylvania Constitution is a living document that has been adapted over the years to meet the challenges of the future and to serve the changing needs of the people of the Commonwealth.

For further information on topics in this chapter, see the following sources in *Key to Further Information:*

The Constitution of the Commonwealth of Pennsylvania

The Pennsylvania Manual

2

The Executive

The executive branch of Pennsylvania government, according to Article IV, Section 1, of the constitution, consists of a governor, lieutenant governor, attorney general, auditor general, and treasurer, who are elected, the Secretary of Education, who is not elected, and "such other offices as the General Assembly may from time to time prescribe." These offices include the departments of the executive branch and many boards and commissions which together perform the executive and administrative work of the Commonwealth. While the constitution outlines the broad powers of the executive branch, the Administrative Code of 1929, as amended, defines the powers and duties of the departments, boards, and commissions. Other laws provide for additional state agencies not included in the code.

The Governor

The governor is the highest elected official in Pennsylvania. The constitution states that "the supreme executive power shall be vested in the gover-

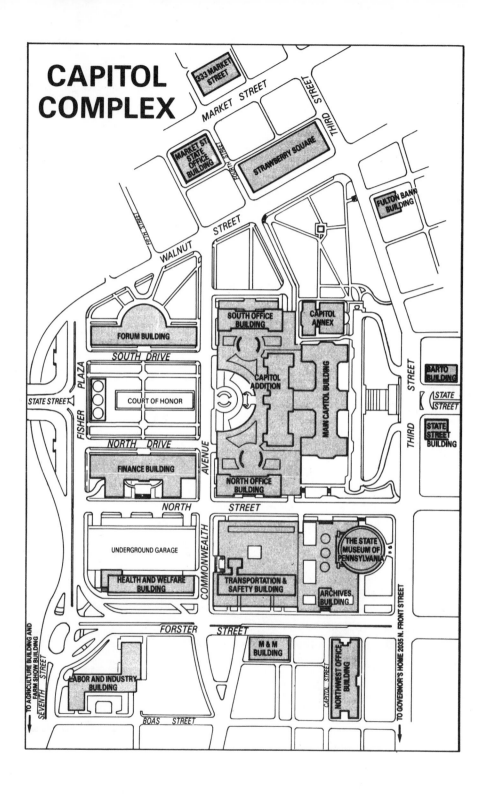

nor, who shall take care that the laws be faithfully executed." As chief executive of the Commonwealth, the governor heads the executive branch with its various departments and agencies, draws up the annual budget, proposes legislation to the General Assembly, and is ultimately responsible for implementing the laws and spending the appropriations passed by the legislature. The governor has the power to appoint, to convene and adjourn the General Assembly, to veto, and to pardon. The governor is commander-in-chief of the Pennsylvania National Guard except when they are called into active federal service.

Term of Office

The governor's four-year term can be extended for one additional successive term. Prior to 1970, a Pennsylvania governor was prohibited from serving a second term.

Qualifications

To qualify for the governorship, an individual must be at least thirty years old, a citizen of the United States, and a resident of Pennsylvania for at least seven years prior to election.

Impeachment

Pennsylvania has no recall provision—the procedure for removal of an official by popular vote—but a governor, or other civil officer, may be impeached by the House of Representatives, which has the sole power of impeachment. All impeachments are tried by the Senate, and a two-thirds majority of those present is necessary for conviction. If convicted, a person is removed from office, barred from holding other office, and could, in addition, be tried in the courts.

Succession

The lieutenant governor succeeds the governor in case of death, resignation, conviction of impeachment, or failure to qualify. If the governor is disabled, the lieutenant governor acts in the governor's place. If the lieutenant governor becomes governor, the president pro tempore of the Senate then becomes lieutenant governor. If there is no lieutenant governor, the president pro tempore of the Senate succeeds to the governorship and a new senator is elected.

The Lieutenant Governor

The lieutenant governor, elected jointly with the governor for a four-year term, carries out the executive and administrative functions of the office. The same qualifications apply to the office of lieutenant governor as to the governor's office.

The lieutenant governor is president of the Senate but has no vote unless the Senate is equally divided. The lieutenant governor may cast a tie-breaking vote on any question except the final passage of a bill. He serves as the governor's representative on various boards and committees and heads the Pennsylvania Energy Office.

In addition to the governor and lieutenant governor, three other officials of the executive branch are elected statewide. They are the attorney general, the auditor general, and the treasurer.

The Attorney General

The attorney general is the Commonwealth's chief legal and law enforcement officer. The Office of Attorney General is an independent department, that is, not under the jurisdiction of the governor since the attorney general is elected directly by the voters.

In 1978, voters approved a constitutional amendment for direct election of the attorney general, which became effective with the 1980 election. Prior to this the attorney general was appointed by the governor and headed the Department of Justice in the governor's cabinet. The effect of the amendment was to separate this office from that of the governor, ensuring more independence.

It is the responsibility of the attorney general to:

- furnish legal advice upon request to the governor or any state agency
- represent the Commonwealth in legal actions brought against it
- defend the constitutionality of state laws
- be responsible for the prosecution of organized crime and public corruption

The Auditor General

The auditor general is the chief auditing officer of the Commonwealth and reviews almost every financial transaction of the state, except those of the General Assembly, the judiciary, the Pennsylvania Turnpike Commission, the State Public School Building Authority, and the State Highway and Bridge Authority.

The auditor general's responsibility is to guarantee that all money to which the Commonwealth is entitled is deposited in the state treasury, and that all public funds are disbursed legally and properly. The auditor general also performs management and compliance audits for some state and local offices.

The office of the Auditor General maintains a toll-free hotline as a public service to Pennsylvanians who may wish to report specific instances of fraud, waste, or mismanagement of state funds.

The Treasurer

The treasurer is the chief executive officer of the Treasury Department and official custodian of most state funds. The treasurer's duties include the receipt and deposit of all state monies; the investment and management of short-term securities; pre-audit of all requisitions for accuracy, legality, and reasonableness; and payment to those authorized to receive Commonwealth funds.

The Office of the State Treasurer was created by the Constitution of 1776. Originally treasurers were elected by the legislature, but the Constitution of 1873 brought about their direct election by the people.

The Governor's Office

All executive or administrative agencies are under the jurisdiction of the governor, except for the elected offices of attorney general, auditor general, and treasurer, who are directly responsible to the voters.

The governor's office includes the immediate working staff of the chief executive. Staff officers may include assistants for legislation, fiscal affairs, government operations, intergovernmental relations, and human resources. Each governor appoints a staff and determines areas of responsibility. The governor's cabinet consists of all appointed department heads; several members of the governor's advisory staff, including the secretaries of administration and budget; and a counsel to the governor. The Office of Administration provides staff assistance to the governor and expedites the operations of the executive branch.

Appointments

The governor appoints the head of each department, known as a secretary, who must be confirmed by the Senate. The secretary serves at the governor's pleasure and is a member of the cabinet. The governor, with the approval of the executive board, appoints and fixes the compensation of all deputies and employees in administrative departments, and has appointing power over all non-civil-service employees. Approximately 32 percent of executive department employees are non-civil service.

Through policy statements and executive orders, the governor establishes direction for all employees and agencies under his jurisdiction.

Other officials appointed by the governor and requiring Senate confirmation are heads of independent boards and commissions, members of departmental boards and commissions, and boards of trustees of state colleges and institutions. More than five hundred other boards, commissions, agencies, and councils exist to which the governor also appoints members, not all of these requiring Senate approval. A two-thirds vote of the Senate is still needed for gubernatorial appointments of judges and for vacancies in other elective offices such as auditor general, state treasurer, and certain other statutorily created offices that the governor is authorized to fill if they are vacated during the term.

The governor must nominate a replacement for gubernatorial appointments within ninety days after a vacancy occurs. If the Senate does not act on the appointment within twenty-five legislative days (days the Senate is actually in session), the nominee takes office as if confirmed. Likewise, if the Senate was in recess or adjourned without setting a date for reassembling and does not act within twenty-five legislative days after its return, the nominee takes office.

Veto Power

All bills, except appropriation bills, must be approved or disapproved as a whole by the governor. In the case of appropriation bills, the governor has a "line" or "item" veto, whereby specific provisions may be vetoed. (In contrast, the President of the United States does not possess this power and must accept or reject an appropriation bill in its entirety with all its amendments.)

If the governor does not sign or veto a bill within ten days, it automatically becomes law. At the end of a legislative session the period is extended to thirty days.

If the governor vetoes a bill, the reasons for the veto are attached and the bill is returned to the legislature. A bill can still become law if both houses override the veto with a two-thirds majority vote of members elected, 34 in the Senate and 136 in the House.

The governor can file objections with the Secretary of the Commonwealth within thirty days after final adjournment. This constitutes a veto that the legislature cannot override.

Budget Making

The governor is responsible for annually presenting a balanced operating budget and a five-year
financial plan to the legislature for its consideration. The budget reflects the governor's priorities
for state government. For the fiscal year which
begins July 1, the initial process begins by August
15 of the previous year, at which time the budget
secretary distributes forms to all departments and
agencies, including the governor, chief clerks of
the General Assembly, and the prothonotaries of
various courts. By January 1 the budget secretary
must submit all information to the governor as the
basis for the next budget.

As soon as possible after the General Assembly
convenes in January, the governor submits the
budget, which includes appropriations required
by the executive, legislative, and judicial branches
of state government, along with revenue estimates
from taxes and other sources.

Judicial Power

The governor has the power to fill vacancies in
judicial offices; remit fines and forfeitures; and
grant reprieves, pardons, and commutation of sentences in all criminal cases except impeachment.
Pardons and commutations, however, may be put
into effect only upon written recommendations of
a majority of the Board of Pardons after a full open
hearing upon due public notice.

Extradition—surrender of a fugitive or prisoner
to another state—requires approval of the state
attorney general and the written order of the governor.

Executive Departments

All executive department heads, with the exception of those elected (attorney general, auditor general, and state treasurer), are appointed by the governor with approval of the Senate. They select their own staffs. Internal functions may be reorganized by the departments with the approval of the Executive Board made up of the heads of the administrative departments and chaired by the governor. Reallocation of functions from one department to another, however, generally requires legislative action.

In establishing a department, the legislature may outline its basic organization, determine its general powers and duties, set limits on its authority, and require certain procedures such as reporting and budgeting. Within this framework, and the policy direction of the governor, each department sets up its own plans of action and each department head has the prerogative to organize the department in a manner that will accomplish its goals.

All executive departments, except those of the attorney general, auditor general, and the state treasurer are responsible to the governor, who may request information from any executive officer or department.

Cabinet-Level Agencies

Each department of the executive branch has numerous boards, commissions, advisory committees, and advisory councils that usually are not independent agencies but report to the heads of the departments and agencies to whom they are responsible.

Department of Aging

The Department of Aging, created in 1978, was established to advance the well-being of Pennsylvania's older citizens, to coordinate administration of federal and state aging programs, and to promote organizations that maximize the independence and involvement of older Pennsylvanians. (See chapters 10, Public Health, and 11, Human Services.)

Department of Agriculture

The Department of Agriculture, established in 1895, has regulatory, administrative, investigative, and educational duties. Its mandate is to encourage and promote agriculture and related industries, to control animal and plant diseases and insect pests, and to safeguard the public against impure or misrepresented foods, feeds, fertilizers, and pesticides. The department also promotes the marketing of Pennsylvania farm products. (See chapters 8, Economic Development, 10, Public Health, and 12, Natural Resources.)

Department of Banking

The Department of Banking enforces and administers laws relating to state chartered banks, building and loan associations, loan companies, consumer discount companies, credit unions, pawnbrokers, and agencies involved in the installment buying of motor vehicles. The department is charged with protecting the interests of depositors, creditors, shareholders, and the public. It guards borrowers against unfair interest rates and other illegal charges.

Department of Commerce/Economic Development Partnership

The Department of Commerce is the chief agency for promoting the administration's economic development strategy to diversify Pennsylvania's economic base. The strategy involves helping traditional industries, stimulating the start-up and growth of small businesses, and selectively recruiting new industry, particularly in the high-growth, advanced technology fields. The goal is to preserve and create jobs for Pennsylvania workers. The department acts as a liaison between business and state government and also promotes foreign trade and port development. The Bureau of Statistics within the department collects data on finances and employment and publishes an annual directory and abstract. (See chapter 8, Economic Development.)

Department of Community Affairs

The Department of Community Affairs, created in 1966, was the first such department in the nation. The department provides financial and technical assistance to local governments and community organizations for a wide variety of local economic and social needs and keeps municipal statistical and financial records. It is the chief advocate for municipal interests in both Harrisburg and Washington, D.C., and provides training programs covering all phases of local government operation. In addition, the Department of Commmunity Affairs concerns itself with housing, recreation, planning, and human resources services at the local level. (See chapter 6, Local Government.)

Department of Corrections

Created in 1984, the Department of Corrections is accountable for the management and supervision of the Commonwealth's adult correctional system. Included are all state correctional institutions and regional facilities, as well as community-oriented pre-release facilities.

Department of Education

The Department of Education is authorized to administer the school laws of Pennsylvania and to assist school districts in conducting their educational programs. (See chapter 9, Education.)

Department of Environmental Resources

The Department of Environmental Resources is responsible for administering environmental laws and standards, overseeing the state's forests and parks, land- and water-management programs, and regulating mining operations. (See chapter 12, Natural Resources.)

Department of General Services

The Department of General Services is the central maintenance, purchasing, publishing, and building construction agency for the executive branch and other divisions of state government. The department is divided into five functional areas: executive, administration, procurement, central services, and public works. It combines the powers and duties of the former Department of Property and Supplies and the General State Authority and was formed as a separate entity in 1975.

Department of Health

The Department of Health is responsible for planning and coordinating the health resources of the Commonwealth. It provides direct services such as public health programs for adults and children, treatment for certain diseases; programs for people with communicable diseases and drug and alcohol abuse problems; and subsidies for research and development. (See chapter 10, Public Health.)

Insurance Department

The Insurance Department enforces the insurance laws of the Commonwealth, examines and supervises domestic insurance companies, settles complaints, regulates insurance rates, licenses Pennsylvania and out-of-state companies, and investigates alleged violations of the law.

Department of Labor and Industry

The Department of Labor and Industry, created in 1913, currently administers programs involving building safety and inspection standards; unemployment compensation, workers' compensation, and vocational rehabilitation; and promotes the health, welfare, and safety of employees. It also enforces the 1986 chemical labeling law (right-to-know law). The department's Bureau of Employment Security operates the state's employment service. (See chapter 8, Economic Development.)

Department of Military Affairs

The Adjutant General's office, located at the Indiantown Gap Military Reservation, directs the Pennsylvania National Guard. Duties of the department include protecting the lives and property of the people of Pennsylvania; preserving peace, order, and public safety; and administering the laws concerned with veterans and their dependents.

Department of Public Welfare

The Department of Public Welfare, established in 1921, administers programs that provide local social services and planning activities for disadvantaged adults, children, and families. The department also distributes federal and state funds to local agencies and provides treatment, care, and support services for both state and community facilities, including those for the mentally ill and retarded. (See section on Public Welfare in chapter 11.)

Department of Revenue

The Department of Revenue collects all tax levies, fees, fines, money for special funds, and other state income. The Secretary of Revenue is responsible for the Pennsylvania lottery. The department prepares an official estimate of the tax yield due the Commonwealth and analyzes its effect on proposed changes in either the laws or taxation.

Department of State

The head of the Department of State is the Secretary of the Commonwealth. Nearly all official gubernatorial transactions go through the office of the Secretary of the Commonwealth. The secretary is custodian of the laws and resolutions passed by the General Assembly and of all proclamations issued by the governor and is keeper of the Great Seal of the Commonwealth. A record of all the governor's official acts is kept in the Department of State. The department also compiles, publishes, and certifies all election returns; furnishes copies of codes to local governments, commissions, and other bodies; issues all commissions to elected and appointed officials; records and prepares for publication all laws passed by the General Assembly; executes corporate and selected noncorporate business laws; administers professional and occupational licensing boards; and regulates boxing and wrestling matches and solicitation activities of charitable organizations. The department includes the Bureau of Elections and the State Athletic Commission.

Pennsylvania State Police

The Pennsylvania State Police, established in 1905, was the first uniformed police organization of its kind in the nation, providing a model for police agencies in other states. The state police provide protection to the large rural areas of the state and gives assistance to local law-enforcement authorities. The department is responsible for aiding the governor in the enforcement of Commonwealth laws and for the preservation of peace and order, detection of crime, and maintenance of criminal records. At the State Police Academy in Hershey, training is provided for state police as well as local police throughout the state.

Department of Transportation

The Department of Transportation is responsible for developing programs to assure adequate, safe, and efficient transportation facilities and services at the lowest reasonable cost to the public. The department issues driver's licenses and motor-vehicle registrations. The Secretary of Transportation oversees the maintenance and operation of state highways, mass transit, rail service, aviation, and bridges. Planning in the department must take into account community and environmental considerations. (See chapter 8, Economic Development.)

Boards and Commissions

Boards and commissions are created, reorganized, or terminated by the legislature or by executive order of the governor. Members of boards and commissions may be appointed by the legislature or the governor with the consent of the Senate, and terms may be up to ten years in length. Boards and commissions, with few exceptions, are financed through the budget submitted by the governor.

The **Governor's Action Center** is the central information and referral agency for the citizens of Pennsylvania. It operates a toll-free number.

The **Council on the Arts,** included in the Governor's Office by legislative act, was created to enrich the artistic and cultural life of Pennsylvanians. The council administers joint federal-state programs that provide services such as the "Artists in the Schools Program."

The **Civil Service Commission** carries out the provisions of the Civil Service Act and its amendments. The commission recruits and examines applicants, certifies lists of names for employment and promotion to appointing authorities, and hears appeals against the actions of appointing authorities.

The **Board of Claims** arbitrates claims against the Commonwealth arising from contracts to which the Commonwealth is a party.

The **Crime Commission** investigates organized criminal activity and public corruption and reports its results to the General Assembly with recommendations for remedial legislative or administrative action.

The **Commission on Crime and Delinquency** is authorized to plan and develop state policy to improve the criminal- and juvenile-justice systems.

The **Emergency Management Agency** (PEMA) is responsible for the planning and coordination of all resources in response to attack and natural or man-made disaster emergencies.

The **Energy Office** develops energy policy and supports the implementation of policy recommendations. Its goal is to ensure energy security through planning, development, and conservation.

The **State Ethics Commission,** created in 1978, administers and enforces the provisions of the Ethics Act so that the activities and financial interests of public office holders, candidates, and certain state employees do not present a conflict of interest with the public trust.

The **Fish Commission** administers and enforces fishing and boating laws, provides for the protection and propagation of aquatic life, and develops and maintains water and related land area to improve public fishing, boating, and other recreational activities. (See chapter 12, Natural Resources.)

The **Game Commission** administers and enforces game laws, manages state game lands, and provides for the protection and propagation of wildlife. (See chapter 12, Natural Resources.)

The **Heritage Affairs Advisory Commission** encourages awareness, understanding, and appreciation of the traditions of Pennsylvania's ethnic population.

The **State System of Higher Education** was established in 1982 to strengthen the state's commitment to excellence in education at the undergraduate and graduate level.

The **Higher Education Assistance Agency** (**PHEAA**) was established to improve the higher education opportunities of Pennsylvania residents by guaranteeing private loans, providing grants, and administering institutional work-study programs and grants to institutions. (See chapter 9, Education.)

The **Governor's Council on the Hispanic Community** is the Commonwealth's advocate agency for Hispanic citizens.

The **Historical and Museum Commission,** an independent administrative board under the governor's jurisdiction, is responsible for the conservation of Pennsylvania's historical heritage. It maintains state archives and administers various museums, and cooperates with local historical societies to promote public interest in Pennsylvania history.

The **Housing Finance Agency** has the power to float mortgage revenue bonds and provides for the construction and substantial rehabilitation of single and multifamily housing for low- to moderate-income families and the elderly.

The **Human Relations Commission,** part of the Governor's Office by legislative act, administers both the Pennsylvania Human Relations Act and the Fair Educational Opportunities Act, which prohibit discrimination because of race, color, religious creed, national origin, age, or sex. The commission investigates complaints of unlawful discrimination; holds hearings on complaints and, where applicable, issues cease and desist orders or secures court orders to ensure compliance with the laws of the Commonwealth; and provides assistance to organizations and industry to obtain voluntary compliance with equal rights legislation.

The **Independent Regulatory Review Commission** oversees and reviews each proposed and existing rule and regulation issued by every department, board, commission, agency, or other authority, except for the legislature, the courts, political subdivisions, municipal or local authorities, or the Fish and Game Commissions.

The **Liquor Control Board,** created in 1933 in response to the repeal of prohibition, operates a system of more than seven hundred state liquor stores and is the largest single purchaser of liquor and wines in the world. The board issues and revokes licenses and permits and enforces liquor laws.

The **Milk Marketing Board** supervises and regulates the milk industry and all matters pertaining to the production, manufacture, storage, processing, transportation, distribution, and sale of milk and milk products; sets prices and licenses all milk dealers, who must be legally bonded; and requires monthly reports from such dealers.

The **Milrite Council** seeks to identify the key barriers to, and opportunities for, economic development and job creation in Pennsylvania and to develop solutions through the cooperation of labor, business, and government.

The **Municipal Retirement Board** has exclusive control and management of retirement funds for municipal employees in Pennsylvania, including municipal police.

The **Board of Probation and Parole** is authorized to grant or revoke parole and to release certain persons from parole. Extensive hearing procedures ensure that the parolee is given adequate due process.

The **Public School Employees Retirement Board,** an independent administrative board, has exclusive control and management of the retirement fund for public school employees.

The **Public Television Network Commission** operates a public television network system interconnecting all noncommercial TV stations in the state. It awards grants to these stations and distributes federal, state, public, and private funds, ensures freedom in programming, and prevents misuse of the network for political or other propaganda purposes.

The **Public Utility Commission (PUC)**, an independent quasi-judicial agency created by legislative act in 1937, regulates the rates and services of approximately seven thousand utilities in Pennsylvania, including natural and manufactured gas, telephone, telegraph, electricity, steam, water, sewage collection and disposal, common carriers of passenger or property, and gas and oil pipeline transmission. It has the power to enforce the safety and reliability of customer service. The PUC budget is paid for by consumers of utility services.

The **Securities Commission** is responsible for the state securities laws.

The **State Employees' Retirement Board** has exclusive control and management of retirement funds for state employees.

The **State Tax Equalization Board** annually determines the state's aggregate market value of assessed taxable real property to be used in settling the amount of subsidies to school districts and support of public libraries, community colleges, and the overall tax limitations in political subdivisions and school districts.

The **Turnpike Commission** was created in 1937 with authority to construct, finance, operate, and maintain a toll highway that now extends 470 miles across the state. The commission is a government corporation, financed with revenue bonds, not state funds.

The **Commission for Women,** part of the Governor's Office by executive order, functions as an advocate of women's issues and a clearinghouse for complaints or questions about sex discrimination.

Joint Interstate or Federal-Interstate Bodies

In order to promote shared interests and encourage mutual cooperation, Pennsylvania has entered into a number of interstate compacts and agreements with bordering states. Pennsylvania joins with the federal government and other states in legal arrangements or formal bodies to foster continued planning and protection of common resources and to discourage fragmentation and duplication. Some of these are: Delaware River Basin Compact, Delaware River Joint Toll Bridge Commission, Delaware Valley Urban Area Compact, Atlantic States Marine Fisheries Compact, Interstate Compact for Education, Great Lakes Basin Compact, Interstate Compact to Conserve Oil and Gas, Ohio River Valley Sanitation Compact, Susquehanna River Basin Compact, Wheeling Creek Watershed Protection and Flood Prevention District Compact, Appalachian Regional Commission, Appalachian States Low Level Radioactive Waste Compact, and the Interstate Commission on the Potomac River Basin.

Authorities

Authorities may be defined as government-owned corporations created by legislation at the state or local level, with rules set by the law that created them.

Not all of the Pennsylvania institutions with the name "authority" meet the general definition. Two that do not are the Minority Business Development Authority, which is funded by legislative appropriations, and the now-inactive Civil Disorder Authority. Moreover, two "agencies," the Housing Finance Agency and the Higher Education Assistance Agency (PHEAA), meet the definition of an authority without the title, as do two "commissions," the Turnpike Commission and the Delaware River Joint Toll Bridge Commission.

Authorities are formed to acquire, construct, improve, maintain, or operate projects, and to borrow money and issue bonds to finance them. The authority boards appoint their own executive directors and fix compensation for their employees. Board members receive no compensation but may be reimbursed for expenses incurred in the performance of their duties. Listed below are several representative state authorities. (See chapter 6, Local Government.)

The **General State Authority** was created originally to construct, improve, equip, furnish, maintain, acquire, and operate state buildings, with the projects financed through the sale of general obligation bonds. Its duties and powers are now in the Department of General Services, but the authority continues to function as an independent public corporation until the outstanding debt from bonds sold to finance earlier projects is satisfied in 1997.

The **Higher Educational Facilities Authority** issues and sells bonds for facilities for any nonprofit college or university in Pennsylvania. Facilities that are used for sectarian or religious purposes or universities that have discriminatory admission procedures are excluded.

The **State Highway and Bridge Authority** finances construction improvements, maintenance, and operation of bridges, highways, viaducts, toll bridges, roadside rests, tunnels, maintenance sheds, offices, and garages.

The **State Public School Building Authority** finances a wide variety of school projects. It reviews plans, enters into construction contracts, advises and inspects buildings during the construction period, and leases a facility to a school district at a rental sufficient to repay the bonds in forty years. Authority to review its program is vested in the Department of Education.

Sunshine Act

In 1986 the legislature passed Act 388, the Sunshine Act, which guarantees the public the right to be present at all meetings of government agencies and to observe the deliberation, policy formulation, and decision making of the democratic process. Adequate notice of the time and place of the meetings must be given to the public. The law states that this right is vital to the enhancement and proper functioning of the democratic process.

Exceptions to the law are caucuses, ethics committee meetings, conferences, and executive sessions held to discuss employment or employee evaluation or certain other specific matters.

Sunset Act   Under terms of the Sunset Act of 1981, each government department and agency must be reviewed
periodically to determine whether it should continue its operation or be terminated. A committee
of the General Assembly, the Legislative Budget
and Finance Committee, bases its recommenda-
tion on these criteria:

- whether termination would significantly harm
  or endanger the public health, safety, or welfare
- whether there is overlap or duplication by
  other agencies
- whether there is a more economical way of
  accomplishing the objectives of the agency
- whether there is a demonstrated need, based
  on service to the public, for continuing exis-
  tence of the agency
- whether the operation of the agency has been
  in the public interest
- whether the agency has encouraged public participation in the making of its rules and decisions or whether the agency has permitted
  participation solely by the persons it regulates
- whether there is an alternate, less restrictive
  method of providing the same service to the
  public.

For further information on topics in this chapter,
see the following sources in *Key to Further Information:*

Commonwealth Telephone Directory

The Pennsylvania Manual

Administrative Code of Pennsylvania

3

The General Assembly

The Pennsylvania legislature was established as a lawmaking body in 1776 by the first state constitution. Originally unicameral, the General Assembly became bicameral under the second constitution of 1790 and has been composed of two houses ever since. Every citizen is represented in both houses. Today the legislature consists of a 50-member Senate and 203-member House of Representatives and is the second largest state legislature. Only New Hampshire has more legislators.

The tenth amendment to the United States Constitution provides that powers not delegated to the United States or prohibited to the states are reserved to the states or to the people. Thus the powers of a state are residual. The United States Constitution allows the federal government to coin money, sign treaties, raise armies, and make war, but the residual power permits the states great latitude in other areas.

The Pennsylvania General Assembly, for example, may adopt laws and programs affecting public health, education, welfare, and safety. It can raise revenue, pass laws relating to classes of local government, and confirm, remove, or impeach public officials within the state. It may propose constitutional amendments. In effect, the legislature attempts to promote an orderly society by exercising its lawmaking powers.

Members of the General Assembly

The legislator is

- a policymaker and a leader
- a lawmaker who votes on major bills affecting the entire state and minor bills on single issues affecting only local districts
- an overseer who checks on the spending and the progress of the executive branch
- a representative of his or her district and of individual constituents in their dealings with state government
- a representative of a political party

Qualifications

State senators must be twenty-five years old and representatives twenty-one. They must be citizens of the United States, inhabitants of Pennsylvania for four years, and residents of their own districts for one year. They must reside in the district from which they are elected as long as they serve as the district's representative.

While serving in the General Assembly, legislators may not be appointed or elected to any other state or federal governmental office to which a fee, salary, or perquisite is attached. They are not eligible to hold office if convicted of embezzlement, bribery, perjury, or other infamous crime.

Elections

One legislator is elected from each of the 203 districts at the fall general election in even-numbered years. Representatives are elected every two years; senators, every four years. Senatorial terms are staggered, with half of the members elected every two years.

Salaries

The Pennsylvania Constitution specifically states that legislators may not vote themselves a pay raise during the term for which they are elected. Legislators have on occasion voted themselves additional expense allowances that in the subsequent term became part of their salary. As an example, in 1988 the annual salary of members of the legislature was $35,000, with an unvouchered expense allowance of $12,000. This unvouchered allowance was added to the salary base when the 1988 term was completed for an annual salary of $47,000. In addition, legislators receive a clerical and office allowance, an accountable expense allowance, and mileage for one round trip to Harrisburg each session week. If committees meet when the General Assembly is not in session, each legislator involved is allowed *per diem* expenses. Legislative leaders receive additional salary plus expenses. Pennsylvania legislators are among the highest paid legislators in the nation.

Apportionment

Pennsylvania is divided into 50 senatorial districts and 203 representative districts that must be compact, contiguous, and nearly equal in population. Unless absolutely necessary, no county, city, incorporated town, borough, township, or ward is to be divided.

Reapportionment is required every ten years following the federal census and is the task of a legislative reapportionment commission. The majority and minority leaders of each house are members of the commission, which jointly selects the fifth member as chair. If they fail to select a chair within forty-five days of their appointment, the Supreme Court of Pennsylvania must appoint one within the next thirty days. The commission must file a preliminary plan within ninety days of the appointment of the chair. If it fails to do so, the Supreme Court itself will reapportion the state senatorial and representative districts. Reapportionment, based on the 1980 census, resulted in each senator representing a population of approximately 237,000 and each representative about 58,000.

Legislative Sessions

The General Assembly is a continuing body during the two-year term for which members of the House of Representatives are elected. The term is divided into two one-year sessions, each one with a different number. (The 172nd regular session convened in January 1988.) In the past, legislators completed their work in a few months and returned to their jobs and homes. Now sessions usually last throughout the year, interrupted only by recesses for holidays or campaigns for reelection.

Special sessions may be called by the governor upon petition of a majority of the members elected to each house or if the governor believes public interest requires it. The governor may also, by proclamation, convene the Senate in special session for the transaction of executive business. Each special session may deal only with subjects designated in the proclamation. These sessions can coincide with regular sessions, with certain hours or days delegated to the work of the special session.

The chief clerk of the House and Senate and the secretary of the Senate, along with other officers, are selected by the members of each house on the opening day of each session. These officers are not members of the General Assembly. The chief clerks are responsible for the administrative operations of the legislature and are responsible to the Speaker and the president pro tempore.

Legislative Procedures

Legislative procedures are determined by a variety of factors: constitutional mandates, legal statutes, rules adopted by each house, agreement of the caucuses, and tradition.

Each house is permitted by the state constitution to determine its rules of procedures and must keep a journal of its proceedings. Their sessions are open to the public, and neither can adjourn for more than three days without the consent of the other. Each is empowered to enforce obedience to its process; to protect its members against bribes, violence, or private solicitation; to punish members or others for contempt or disorderly behavior in its presence; and to expel a member by a two-thirds majority vote.

Every member is privileged from arrest except for treason, felony, or violation of oath while at the sessions themselves or going to and coming from them. No member may be sued or otherwise questioned about a speech or debate made on the floor.

The Legislature and the Executive Branch

In describing the division of power in government, it is customary to say that the legislature makes the laws and the executive administers them. In actual practice the executive and legislative branches often work together on shaping legislation. Some legislative ideas originate with the governor or within agencies and departments of the executive branch. Other legislation may originate in either house of the General Assembly. Departments may aid legislators in the preparation of proposed legislation or may furnish information to legislative committees.

The legislature and the governor have certain constitutional checks on each other's activities. The governor may

- veto any bill passed by the legislature
- veto parts of individual appropriation bills
- make certain interim appointments when the Senate is not in session
- call special sessions of the legislature and set their agenda
- adjourn the General Assembly for up to four months when the two houses disagree over adjourning

The legislature may

- override the governor's veto with a two-thirds majority of members elected to each house
- levy or not levy taxes and appropriate money to run the government

- approve executive appointments while the Senate is in session
- impeach and convict the governor
- establish executive departments and assign their general duties

The constitution mandates that each year the governor submit both a balanced budget and a capital budget to the General Assembly for the following fiscal year. The operating budget appropriations passed by the General Assembly may not exceed the actual or estimated revenues plus any surplus in the current year. The General Assembly must also adopt a capital budget.

The General Assembly controls procedures for setting judges' salaries, which must not be decreased while a judge holds office. The General Assembly is empowered to change the number and boundaries of the judicial districts with the advice and consent of the Supreme Court of Pennsylvania. The General Assembly sets salaries of the district justices. The Senate approves the governor's appointments of justices, judges, and district magistrates to fill vacancies. The courts interpret the meaning and determine the constitutionality of laws passed by the legislature. They may also hear cases involving the legislative process itself.

The Legislature and the Judicial Branch

The presiding officer of the Senate is the lieutenant governor, or if the lieutenant governor is absent, the president pro tempore. In the House, the Speaker presides. The House elects a Speaker every other year for two years at the beginning of

Organization of the General Assembly

each regular session in odd-numbered years. The Senate elects a president pro tempore every year at the beginning of each regular session. These two leaders are the choice of the majority caucus in each house. The Speaker of the House and the president pro tempore of the Senate are both responsible to the entire house and not only to members of their own political party.

The duties of presiding officers in both houses are similar. They

- preside over their respective bodies, preserve order and decorum, and decide all points of order
- refer all bills to committees and appoint committee chairpersons
- sign all bills in the presence of their respective houses before these bills are sent to the governor to be signed into law
- appoint all employees of their respective houses

Party Caucuses

A caucus is a closed meeting of all the members of the same political party in one house of the legislature. Following the general election and prior to the beginning of the two-year term, the political parties of each house meet in caucus to select their leaders. Each party caucus chooses a floor leader, a whip, a caucus chairman, and a caucus secretary.

As a rule, the leader of the caucus is the main party spokesperson on the floor of the house for positions agreed upon by the caucus, rarely speaking as an individual member. One of the chief functions of the caucus is to provide its members with information about bills so that policy may be developed and strategy planned to support or oppose legislation. The role of caucuses is one of the most important elements in the passage or defeat of bills in the Pennsylvania legislature.

The caucus system has a number of advantages and disadvantages. Caucuses promote party discipline, eliminate factions, and increase the responsiveness of the two-party system. They provide a forum for education and compromise without publicity. The press and public are not permitted to attend the party caucus; however, legislative staff may be present. Caucuses decide which bills should have priority, weed out less important bills, and dispose of procedural matters that could be very time-consuming.

The whip, who is responsible for delivering individual votes, can employ several tactics as leverage. These include the threat of social ostracism, poor committee assignments, withholding support at election time, detaining bills in committee, and reserving support for the member's district. These pressures, however, are only effective when applied sparingly. When sizable opposition surfaces within the caucus, then discussion, negotiation, and compromise are the usual solutions.

Despite their advantages, caucuses also have some negative effects. The independence of individual members may be lessened, a few individuals can exercise control, and floor sessions can become rubber stamps for caucus decisions reached without public knowledge.

Types of Committees

The legislature has established various committees:

- Standing committee, operating throughout the session to review, hold hearings, and report to the floor on bills
- Interim committee, appointed for specific work and meeting between legislative sessions
- Conference committee, appointed to resolve differences between House- and Senate-passed versions of a bill
- Select or special study committee, appointed for a specific purpose with a definite time limit
- Joint committee, a committee of both houses serving together
- Committee of the whole, the entire membership of a house sitting as a committee in order to discuss a question more fully

When the legislature organizes for work, committee chairmen are selected and members are assigned to committees. The president pro tempore appoints both the chair and the members of Senate committees. In the House, the Committee on Committees, composed of the Speaker, ten majority members, and five minority members, appoints legislators to committees and subcommittees. The Speaker appoints the chair and vice-chair of each standing committee and subcommittee.

In 1987–88 there were twenty-three standing committees in the House. Standing committees in the House have fourteen members from the majority party and nine from the minority party with the following exceptions: Appropriations Committee—nineteen majority party members, ten minority party; Committee on Rules—nine majority, five minority; Ethics Committee—four majority, four minority.

The Senate, with twenty-one standing committees, does not follow the majority-minority ratio of the House in its committee assignments. Its rules state that the composition of each standing committee shall reasonably reflect the party composition of the Senate membership.

Two important committees in both houses are the Rules Committee and the Appropriations Committee. The Rules Committee establishes the rules of each house and handles policy bills, resolutions, and bills of particular importance. The Appropriations Committee holds hearings on the budget submitted by the governor and reports a budget bill to the floor. All bills that require an appropriation must pass through the Appropriations Committee for a fiscal note, that is, a specific cost figure. Other bills are referred to the committee for evaluation of fiscal impact.

In general, the work of standing committees is to determine policy and analyze bills, to settle details, to examine previous laws and judicial decisions affecting the proposals, to designate administrative responsibility for carrying out the purposes of bills, and to draft and approve bills and their amendments. Committees may hold public hearings and conduct investigations.

Committee Procedures

Once a bill is in committee, the committee has full power over it. The committee chair is able to select which bills will be studied and to decide when the committee will meet. In the House a majority of the members of a commmittee may request that a bill be considered. If the chair refuses, a majority vote of all members of the committee can require the chair to act. In the House it takes at least ten votes to discharge a bill from committee, except in the Appropriations Committee, where fourteen votes are needed. In the Senate it takes a majority vote of the quorum to discharge a bill from committee. In both houses a quorum is necessary for a committee meeting to properly conduct the commmittee's business.

There is no rule in either house requiring the reporting of a bill out of committee after a certain period of time. If a bill is in Senate committee less than ten days, it may be discharged by unanimous consent of the Senate. After ten days in a Senate committee and fifteen days in a House committee, however, a bill may be discharged by majority vote of the members elected to that house.

Public hearings may be held in the capital or in various areas of the state. Occasionally, committees of both houses hold joint hearings. The committee invites persons whom it considers qualified to testify on the subject and accepts testimony from a certain number of persons or organizations upon request. The committee may require witnesses to file statements of their testimony in advance.

Staff Support for the General Assembly

Approximately 1,800 General Assembly employees, both full-time and part-time, are divided among the leadership offices, caucuses, service agencies, and standing committees. Attorneys, accountants, and research assistants on the caucus staff also assist some of the committees. None of the General Assembly employees is under civil service. Staff members include the chief clerk of the House, House secretary and House parliamentarian, and the secretary of the Senate, Senate chief clerk, and Senate librarian.

Each committee chair has an office and a secretary. A few representatives share office space and secretarial services. Each state senator has an office and a secretary. The Data Processing Center provides computerized information for bill drafting and prints bills.

Legislative Service Agencies

Legislative service agencies offer additional legislative help and provide oversight functions. The oldest of the agencies, the Legislative Reference Bureau, drafts or checks all bills submitted by members of the legislature. Legislative commissions, with members from both houses, employ an executive director and full-time staff to provide research support services to legislators in key areas.

The Local Government Commission drafts and considers bills on local government. It is composed of ten legislators, five from each house. Most of the members serve on local government committees in their respective houses.

The Legislative Budget and Finance Committee, composed of six legislators from each house, analyzes the budget submitted by the governor, conducts management studies of funds appropriated by the legislature, and recommends appropriate action. This committee also conducts the review of agencies in accordance with the provisions of the Sunset legislation, requiring periodic justification for the need of all governmental agencies, commissions, and departments.

The Joint State Government Commission is made up of all the members of the legislature. A fifteen-member executive committee consisting of the leadership of both houses conducts the business of the commission. The commission staff includes economists, political scientists, statisticians, and attorneys. It undertakes special studies recommended by the General Assembly and the executive committee, and provides technical services requested by standing committees.

The Joint Legislative Air and Water Pollution Control and Conservation Committee, composed of nine members from each house, reviews and studies environmental laws and regulations. The committee can propose changes in present legislation or draft new legislation.

The Legislative Audit Advisory Committee, with two members from each house and three from the public, hires an accounting firm to audit all expense accounts of the House, Senate, and committees and presents an annual audit report.

Lobbyists

A lobbyist is a person representing a special interest who tries to influence a legislator in favor of, or against, particular legislation. It should be noted that in addition to lobbyists employed by corporations, unions, professional associations, or other organizations, virtually every state agency and every department of the executive branch of state government has legislative liaisons who engage in some kind of lobbying activity.

In the nineteenth century lobbyists were considered the purveyors of bribes and the buyers of votes. Although the public still tends to view lobbyists with suspicion for advocating a narrow interest, lobbyists also provide reasoned opinions, information, and technical assistance to legislators. They can help legislators understand issues while they are promoting their special interests. Since legislators hear from numerous lobbying groups, including citizen and volunteer lobbyists such as the League of Women Voters, they can weigh a wide range of arguments before making their own decisions.

A lobbyist must register with the secretary of the Senate and chief clerk of the House of Representatives within five days after beginning lobbying activity, if the lobbyist receives compensation in excess of $500 per year or spends or incurs obligations on behalf of any one person in excess of $300 in any month. Expenses include meals, entertainment, and the cost of communication to the General Assembly or any agency. In addition, the lobbyist must file a financial statement twice a year showing expenses and obligations incurred during the previous six months. Regulations covering lobbyists' activities are included in Act 212 of 1976.

Legislation

A number of important mandatory provisions regarding legislative procedures are included in the constitution of Pennsylvania:

- No law may be passed except by bill, and no bill may be amended to change its original purpose.
- No bill may have more than one subject except a general appropriation bill.
- All bills must be referred to committee before being considered by either house.
- Each bill must be considered on three different days.
- All amendments to bills must be printed before a vote or before the final vote on the entire bill is taken.
- All bills require a roll call vote (by name in the Senate or by electronic voting machine in the

House), and the names and votes must be recorded in the journal.

- Presiding officers must sign all bills and resolutions in the presence of their respective houses.
- If the governor vetoes a bill, a two-thirds majority of members elected to each house is required to override the veto.
- The general appropriation bill includes monies appropriated for the executive, legislative, and judicial branches for the public debt and public schools. All other appropriation bills, generally termed "nonpreferred," must be separate bills, one to a subject.
- All revenue bills originate in the House of Representatives.
- Appropriation bills may originate in either house. Passage normally requires a majority of elected members; nonpreferred bills, however, such as those appropriating money for state-related institutions, require a two-thirds vote of the members elected to each house.
- Members may not raise the salary or extend the term of office of any public officer, including themselves, while in office.

Passage of a Bill

A bill passes through various stages before it becomes law:

- introduction and referral to committee
- committee examination
- review by caucus
- three considerations and passage by one house
- referral to the other house where it must follow the four previous steps

- adjustment in conference committee if necessary
- signing by the leaders of both houses
- action by the governor

Introduction of a Bill

Before a bill is introduced, the sponsor's idea must be translated into legal language, a task frequently performed by the Legislative Reference Bureau. The sponsor tries to attract the widest possible bipartisan and leadership assistance. In the Senate, bills are introduced by the sponsor standing in place and reading the title to the presiding officer, who assigns it to committee. In the House, bills are handed to the chief clerk. At the end of the day the Speaker assigns bills to committees. In both houses the journal of the following day carries the bill's committee assignment, following which the bill is numbered and printed for the legislature and the public. Between three and four thousand bills are introduced in each session of the legislature, but only a fraction ever become law. Much of the legislation consists of necessary state business. Of the many bills introduced, only a relatively small number are controversial or partisan.

In Committee

By means of the committee system, the large number of bills is reduced to a manageable number. Committees may select any of the following actions:

HOW A BILL BECOMES LAW

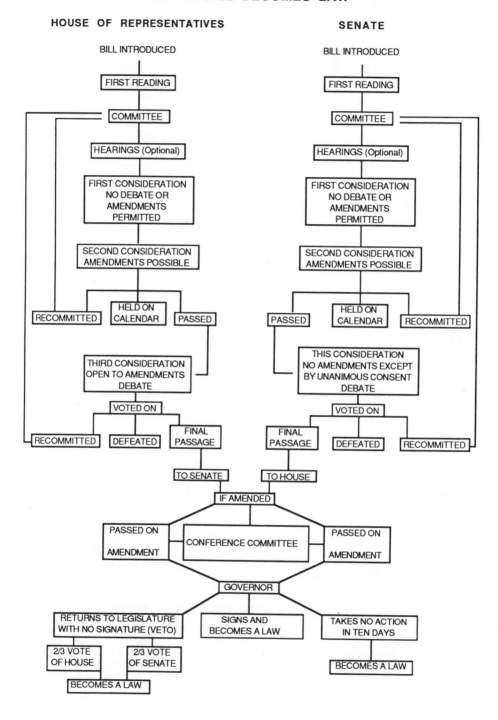

- report the bill favorably with no suggested amendments
- report the bill as amended
- report the bill unfavorably with negative recommendations
- take no action

In Caucus

Before a bill goes to the floor for consideration, each party caucus has an opportunity to discuss it, to explain it to those who may be unaware of its provisions, and to agree upon party positions and strategy. Members learn who is interested in the bills and what the effect will be on their own home districts.

Caucuses review the bills on each day's calendar, after which the leadership of both parties meets with the presiding officer of the house involved to review the caucuses' decisions. The presiding officer can then anticipate what actions might be taken once the session begins.

Caucus activities are usually more important and time-consuming for the majority caucus than for the minority. Complete agreement in the majority party can assure the passage or defeat of a bill in one of the houses.

On the Floor

If a bill is amended in committee, it is reprinted and given a new printer's number. Although a bill retains its assigned bill number as it passes through the legislature, its printer's number changes each time it is amended.

Every bill must be considered on three different

legislative days. First consideration is usually given a bill on the day it is reported from committee. No amendments or debate are permitted from the floor at this time. A bill then moves into second consideration on the calendar, at which point amendments and debate are permitted. Once past this stage a bill is listed for third consideration on the calendar. The bill may be amended in the House, but it may not be voted upon until it is reprinted to include the amendment. There can be no amendment in the Senate during third consideration unless by unanimous consent.

After the conclusion of debate and amendment, the presiding officer announces that the bill is ready for final passage and a roll call vote is taken.

Passage and Referral to Other House

Final passage of a bill requires a majority vote of the members elected to each house. This is known as a constitutional majority and is 102 votes in the House or 26 votes in the Senate. A two-thirds vote of the members elected to each house (34 in the Senate and 136 in the House) is required for certain matters. These include overriding the governor's veto and final passage of nonpreferred appropriation bills for such institutions as state-related universities and museums. Once a bill passes one house, it is sent by messenger to the other house, where the process is repeated.

If the bill is defeated in the second house, it dies. If amended, it is returned to the house where it originated for concurrence. When the originating house does not concur in the amendments, a conference committee of members of both houses is appointed to work out differences. The committee is composed of two majority members and one minority member from each house appointed by the presiding officer. A majority of the conferees from each house must approve the conference committee report, which is then returned to the house where the bill originated. That house votes first, and, if approved, the bill is again sent to the other house for concurrence. A conference committee report is not amendable.

Bills may be reconsidered in both houses and may also be recalled from either house or from the governor's desk.

There is another legislative process used occasionally that limits floor consideration to a large extent. A bill that has passed one house may be amended so completely that the original bill is deleted and an entire new bill is inserted in its place. This is permissible as long as the "amendments" deal with the same subject as the original bill. If the other house passes such an amended bill, it then goes to a conference committee, which has final say on the bill. This maneuver bypasses the rest of the legislative process and eliminates discussion and possible changes in the bill.

Bills may be introduced at any time. Those not passed die at the end of the two one-year sessions.

Action by the Governor

After the leaders of both houses sign the bill it goes to the State Department for recording. The State Department then transmits it to the governor. The General Counsel's Office then reviews the legality of the bill for the governor. If the governor signs the bill, it becomes law and is known as an act. The act returns to the State Department, where the Secretary of the Commonwealth verifies it as a true and correct copy as printed, assigns it an act number, and arranges for its filing. The Department of State then forwards the law to the Legislative Reference Bureau, where it is prepared for printing.

The governor can veto the bill. To override the veto a two-thirds majority of both houses is necessary. In rare cases a bill may become a law without the governor's signature if the governor does not act on it within ten days after it has been received, or thirty days after adjournment of the General Assembly.

Citizen Participation

The League of Women Voters encourages citizens to make their views known by writing or visiting their legislators. Citizens can keep abreast of issues in which they have special interest through the local offices of their legislators, where staff is available to provide service and answer questions.

Sunshine Act

The Open Meeting Law, known as the Sunshine Act, passed in 1974 and amended in 1986, not only guarantees the right of citizens to attend meetings of state agencies at which agency business is discussed or acted upon, but it ensures that adequate notice of such meetings will be published. The law covers the General Assembly and agencies of the executive branch and any board, council, commission, or committee of any political subdivision of the Commonwealth. No formal action by an agency is valid unless taken during a public meeting. Exempt from open public meetings are executive sessions whose topics are specified in the law, and political caucuses.

For further information on topics in this chapter, see the following sources in *Key to Further Information*:

The Legislative Journal

The Legislative Directory

The Legislative Reference Bureau

4

The Courts and the Administration of Justice

Courts interpret the constitution and the laws. They protect the rights of individuals against violations committed by others and by various levels and divisions of government.

States are free to structure their judicial systems within limits set down by the United States Constitution, most notably that section of the Fourteenth Amendment that reads:

> No state shall . . . deprive any person of life, liberty, or property, without due process of law, nor deny to any person within its jurisdiction the equal protection of the laws.

Article I of the Pennsylvania Constitution, the Declaration of Rights, protects the rights of individuals against arbitrary action by the government and provides for the rights of the accused.

Courts of the Commonwealth   Pennsylvania's judicial system derives its authority from Article V, Section 1, of the state constitution, which provides for a unified court system consisting of the Supreme Court, Superior Court, Commonwealth Court, Court of Common Pleas, and such other courts as provided by law.

The General Assembly is authorized to establish additional courts or divisions or to abolish any statutory courts. It determines the number of judges for all except the Supreme and Superior Courts and also determines the jurisdiction of each court.

Jurisdiction of a court refers to the kinds of cases that a court has a right to hear. Original jurisdiction applies to a court that hears cases being brought to court for the first time. Appellate jurisdiction is the right of a court to hear appeals of rulings made in a lower court.

Pennsylvania's unified court system became a reality in 1968, when the voters approved the judicial revisions to the constitution proposed by the Constitutional Convention of 1967–68. Prior to 1968 each court operated independently in a manner determined by its judges. There was no centralized administration, no common method of record-keeping, and no authority for shifting judges according to the size of caseloads. Now all courts from special courts through the state Supreme Court are part of an integrated, unified system under the administration of the state Supreme Court through the Administrative Office of Pennsylvania Courts.

Other reforms in the 1968 Constitution include mandatory retirement of all state judges at age seventy, the establishment of a Judicial Inquiry and Review Board, and a constitutional guarantee for the right of appeal in all cases, including those involving minor courts not of record (see minor judiciary, below) and state agencies.

The Courts of the Commonwealth

SUPREME COURT
10-year Term
7 Justices
Number set by
Constitution

COMMONWEALTH COURT
10-year Term
9 Judges
Number set by law

SUPERIOR COURT
10-year Term
15 Judges
Number set by law
and Constitution

COURTS OF COMMON PLEAS
10-year Term
Currently 60 districts
for 67 counties
Number of judges and divisions
for each court set by law

MINOR JUDICIARY

DISTRICT COURTS
6-year Term
One per district

PHILADELPHIA TRAFFIC COURT
6-year Term
Number of judges
set by law

PHILADELPHIA MUNICIPAL COURT
6-year term
Number of judges
set by law

PITTSBURGH MAGISTRATES COURT
4-year term
Appointed by
Mayor

Supreme Court

Pennsylvania's Supreme Court, the oldest appellate court in the United States, was created in 1722 by the Provincial Assembly. It was incorporated into the court system in the constitution of 1776.

The highest judicial authority in the Commonwealth, the Supreme Court is staffed by seven justices elected for ten-year terms. The number of justices is set by the constitution and the justice with the longest continuous service on the court is the chief justice.

The Supreme Court hears appeals from other state courts and has some original jurisdiction. It also may assume jurisdiction by its own motion, or by petition of any party, over an issue of immediate public importance that is before any court or justice of the peace. This authority is known as "extraordinary jurisdiction."

Direct appeals from Courts of Common Pleas to the Supreme Court include all cases of felonious homicide and constitutional questions. Appeals from the Commonwealth Court to the Supreme Court encompass any matter originating in the Commonwealth Court. The Supreme Court may hear any other decision of the Commonwealth Court or the Superior Court upon allowance by any two Supreme Court justices.

Superior Court

The Pennsylvania Superior Court, an intermediate appellate court, was established in 1895 by the General Assembly to reduce the workload of the Supreme Court. The number of judges is set by the constitution. The Superior Court consists of fifteen judges elected for ten-year terms, with the president judge elected for a five-year term by the other members of the court.

The Superior Court hears all appeals from Courts of Common Pleas unless they have been assigned to the Supreme Court or Commonwealth Courts. Such appeals include all criminal cases except those involving felonious homicide. The Superior Court has some original jurisdiction, but it is very limited.

Commonwealth Court

The nine-member Pennsylvania Commonwealth Court was created as a separate entity by the legislature during the 1968 revisions to the state constitution. The president judge is the judge with the longest continuous service.

The Court generally hears cases relating to the activities of the Commonwealth and its agencies. Its original jurisdiction includes civil actions against the Commonwealth or any of its officers. Notable exceptions exist in the areas of eminent domain (the right of a government to take private property for public use) or in habeas corpus (the right of a citizen to obtain a writ by which to test the legality of his or her imprisonment).

The appellate jurisdiction of the court covers appeals from Courts of Common Pleas, except where an action is within the jurisdiction of the Supreme or Superior Courts. Such appeals include civil actions and proceedings involving the Commonwealth, criminal actions and proceedings involving state administrative agencies, appeals concerning local administrative agencies, all eminent-domain proceedings, and interpretation of acts of the General Assembly, home-rule charters, or local ordinances or resolutions.

Court of Common Pleas: Judicial Districts

The Court of Common Pleas is primarily a trial court with original jurisdiction on most serious criminal and civil cases not specifically assigned to another court. Matters having to do with inheritance, divorce, child custody, and adoption are also heard in this court.

The number of judges for each Court of Common Pleas and the assignment of judicial districts are determined by the legislature. Judges are elected for ten-year terms and the judge with the longest continuous service presides as president judge, except in districts of more than seven judges, where the members of the court select a president judge for a five-year term.

Currently the sixty-seven counties of Pennsylvania are divided into sixty judicial districts. Seven of these districts are composed of two counties (Cameron and Elk, Columbia and Montour, Forest and Warren, Franklin and Fulton, Juniata and Perry, Snyder and Union, Sullivan and Wyoming); the remainder consist of a single county each. Each judicial district has one Court of Common Pleas, with divisions as provided by the legislature. These divisions may include Civil, Criminal, Juvenile, Family, and Orphans' Courts.

The number and boundaries of judicial districts may be changed by the General Assembly only with the advice and consent of the Supreme Court. Salaries for justices and judges are set by the legislature.

Court Officers

One clerk and one prothonotary are elected in each judicial district. In some counties the offices of clerk of court and prothonotary are combined. In counties with home rule they are designated the clerk of judicial records. These offices maintain and are responsible for court records, books, and dockets. The prothonotary keeps all records involving litigation. Some counties designate the register of wills as the clerk of Orphans' Court ex officio. Both positions are salaried.

The special courts, commonly known as the minor judiciary, include district justice, municipal, traffic, and magistrate courts. These courts do not use juries. They are "courts of first instance" and "courts not of record." If a case initiated in the minor courts goes on to higher levels of the court system, no verbatim record from the first court follows and the case is heard as if it were new. In general, the jurisdiction extends to traffic violations, summary offenses, vehicle-code violations, landlord and tenant matters, and criminal offenses where little or no imprisonment is involved. A citizen may use the district court as a small-claims court to recover amounts totaling up to $4,000 exclusive of interest and costs. District justices also have jurisdiction to issue warrants and to hold preliminary arraignments and preliminary hearings in all criminal cases.

Minor Judiciary

District Justices

Reform of the minor judiciary was approved by the voters in 1967–68. The changes included provision for compulsory training and examination of district justices, abolition of the fee system in favor of salaried positions, reduction in the number of minor courts, and supervision by the state Supreme Court as part of the unified court system.

The number and boundaries of magisterial districts are established by the Supreme Court or by Courts of Common Pleas under the direction of the Supreme Court; as of 1987 there were 553 districts.

District justices, sometimes still referred to as justices of the peace, squires, magistrates, or aldermen, must either be lawyers or have taken a training course and passed a qualifying examination, unless they have served a previous term as justice of the peace. All fines collected must go to the appropriate authority as designated by law.

Philadelphia Municipal and Traffic Courts

The Philadelphia Municipal Courts follow somewhat different rules, and court records may follow to a higher court. The court has jurisdiction over minor civil and criminal cases. Twenty-two judges, who must be lawyers, are elected for six-year terms. Philadelphia Traffic Court has exclusive jurisdiction of all summary offenses that are committed within the limits of the city and county of Philadelphia. It consists of six judges, elected for six-year terms, who must either complete a course of training and pass an examination or be members of the bar. The number of judges in both courts is determined by the legislature.

Magistrates, City of Pittsburgh

Similar to district justices of the peace, the Pittsburgh magistrates are part of the unified judicial system. The Magistrate Court has six magistrates appointed by the mayor with approval of the city council. They are the only nonelected members of

the judiciary in the state except for interim gubernatorial appointees.

The court has limited criminal and civil jurisdiction over offenses committed within city limits.
The magistrates also sit on the Pittsburgh housing
court and the traffic court, where jurisdiction is
limited to motor-vehicle-code violations. District
justices have concurrent jurisdiction, along with
police magistrates, within the city.

Constables

The role of the constable is poorly defined. Although one or more constables are elected for a
six-year term from each municipality or each ward
in a city, the constable is not responsible to the
municipal government, the local police, or to any
court officer. In practice, many constables work for
district justices and may serve legal process papers
and warrants, transport prisoners, or conduct
sheriff sales. They may be present or appoint a
deputy to be present at polling places.

Community Courts

Community courts were authorized as part of the
1968 revisions to the judiciary article of the state
constitution. They may be established by referendum with approval by a majority of the voters in a
judicial district. There are no community courts in
Pennsylvania at this time.

Administration of Courts in Pennsylvania

Under the jurisdiction of the state Supreme Court,
all court administration is coordinated by the Administrative Office of Pennsylvania Courts, located

in Philadelphia. The appointed court administrator, a member of the bar, sets the rules of conduct governing all court personnel. The office keeps records, compiles data for all courts, and maintains accounting and budgetary records. A uniform system of record-keeping makes it possible to transfer records from one court to another in cases where jurisdiction is transferred or appeals are made. The administrator helps to equalize loads by assigning judges where needed.

Financing Courts

A 1987 decision by the Supreme Court ruled that all courts are to be funded by the Commonwealth. Implementation has yet to be determined. Prior to this decision, courts have been financed by state and county appropriations. The county has been primarily responsible for housing and equipping the county courts, including those of district justices, while the state has been responsible for judicial salaries and for financing statewide courts.

State funds for courts are appropriated by procedures similar for other state offices. A budget, prepared for all courts by the court administrator, must be approved by the Supreme Court and the governor and ultimately be submitted to the legislature. Costs and fines collected by the courts are used to offset expenses of these offices in addition to those monies designated for the judiciary in the state budget.

Some salaries, such as those of judges, are set by law; those of the staff are set by the court concerned. At present, the county salary board determines salaries of clerks and assistants. The salaries of district justices are set by the legislature and vary according to the population of the magisterial district.

All justices of the Supreme Court, judges, and district justices are initially elected on a partisan ballot; all except district justices then run for retention on a "yes-no" basis without any political designation and without opposing candidates. Only district justices and Common Pleas Court judges may cross-file for election. Vacancies during terms of office are filled by appointment by the governor with approval of the Senate.

Merit selection refers to a system of judicial selection whereby candidates are recommended to the governor by a selection committee consisting of lawyers and nonlawyers. The merit selection of judges has been a concern of Pennsylvanians for many years. The issue of the appointment of statewide judges by the governor rather than their election was last placed before the voters in 1968 when it was narrowly defeated. A modified merit selection does occur in the event of a vacancy on the court. The governor chooses a replacement from a list of candidates presented by a commission of lawyers and nonlawyers. That individual would then run for a full term on a party ballot in the next election.

In the past, judicial elections were only held in odd-numbered years.

Justices, judges, and district justices must retire at the age of seventy, with retirement benefits provided by law. After that age they may be assigned temporary duty by the Supreme Court.

Justices and judges are prohibited from holding office in political parties or organizations or holding a salaried position at any level of government, except in the armed forces.

Selection and Removal of Judges

Judicial Inquiry and Review Board

The Judicial Inquiry and Review Board recommends to the Supreme Court the suspension, removal, discipline, or compulsory retirement of any judge or justice when it determines there is good cause for such action.

Members of the Judicial Inquiry and Review Board, who serve four-year terms, may not hold office in a political party or organization. Membership consists of three judges from three different Common Pleas Courts and two Superior Court judges, all selected by the Supreme Court. The remaining four members are appointed by the governor: two are members of the bar not serving as judges, and two are lay people. Board hearings, proceedings, and records are confidential. Once the cases reach the Supreme Court, however, the records become public.

Any justice, judge, or district justice who is convicted of misbehavior in office by a court, disbarred by the Supreme Court, or removed under proceedings of the Judicial Inquiry and Review Board, automatically forfeits the judicial office and becomes ineligible for future office. A justice or judge who is retired compulsorily retires with full rights and benefits; the salary of a justice or judge who is suspended or removed ceases from the date of the order. Justices or judges who file for nomination or election to public office other than judicial office automatically forfeit their judicial office.

Impeachment of Judges

Judges may be impeached by the House of Representatives and tried by the Senate. A two-thirds vote is necessary for conviction. Judges continue to hold office until the impeachment charge is settled.

The state constitution guarantees the right to trial by jury. In civil cases the parties may, by agreement, dispense with trial by jury. In 1970 the constitution was amended to permit a verdict in a civil case to be rendered by five-sixths of a jury.

Trials

Juries

Two types of juries function in Pennsylvania: the grand jury and the petit or trial jury. The petit jury sits during the actual trial of a case. The grand jury does not try cases. It considers formal indictments set before it by the district attorney to decide whether testimony shows a *prima facie* case (legally sufficient to establish a case unless disproved) to hold a person for trial. However, a 1973 constitutional amendment allows Courts of Common Pleas, with the approval of the Supreme Court, to provide for the initiation of criminal charges using a district attorney's information (a formal accusation of a crime made by a public officer), rather than by grand-jury indictment. This is the procedure used in most counties in the state. In addition, the grand jury performs special investigations given to it by the court, including those involving criminal charges against public officials on matters of general public significance.

To qualify for jury duty, an individual must be a citizen over the age of eighteen, a resident of the district, and must be able to understand English. Grounds for exemption from jury duty vary from one county to another. Excuses are not automatic and must be requested even by those who ordinarily are exempt, such as ministers, priests, rabbis, doctors, and lawyers. Names of prospective jurors are selected from lists drawn up by elected jury commissioners who use voter registrations, driver registrations, and telephone directories and select prospective jurors at random. Jurors are paid a daily fee plus mileage for the days they serve.

The District Attorney and Public Defender

The district attorney, who is elected, serves as the public prosecutor when state laws are broken. The district attorney signs all bills of indictment presenting information to the grand jury. In counties where a grand jury is no longer used, the district attorney signs an information, which is presented to the Court of Common Pleas at an arraignment to present formal charges to the defendent before he or she pleads guilty or not guilty. The district attorney also conducts all criminal and other prosecutions to which the Commonwealth is a party.

Right to Counsel

According to rulings by the United States Supreme Court, every defendent has a right to counsel; counsel must be provided for those who are too poor to obtain their own. Pennsylvania law requires county governments to set up a public defender's office and appoint a public defender.

Bail

All accused persons, except those accused of first-degree murder, are bailable. The amount of bail bond is fixed in order to ensure the presence of a defendant for trial. The level is determined by several factors: the nature and circumstances of the offense; the stage of the prosecution; the age, residence, employment, financial standing, and family status of the defendant; the defendant's character and reputation, previous criminal record, and mental condition.

Nominal bail requires a fee of one dollar, the defendant's signature, and surety by an official of the court. It may be granted if the offense is a misdemeanor or summary offense, and if the defendant or the defendant's family are known or proven to be responsible and dependable persons. Certain forms of security are accepted as bail: bonds of an authorized surety company or professional bondsman; real estate of the defendant or another person; deposits of cash, certified check, cashier's check, or money order.

Various levels of government, departments, boards, and commissions are involved with the correctional system.

Correctional System

Adult Correctional Institutions

All state adult correctional institutions are administered by the Department of Corrections. Each institution provides a program of vocational and academic training and special programs for prisoners who require them. Pennsylvania maintains fourteen adult state correctional institutions or facilities. Counties are required to maintain county jails for criminals serving sentences of less than two years. Prison custodial officers are recruited through civil service and must be high school graduates.

Juvenile Justice System

Typically persons under the age of eighteen are classified as juveniles by law. County governments in Pennsylvania are responsible for the prevention and treatment of juvenile delinquency. Through the Department of Public Welfare, the Commonwealth financially assists counties in providing programs for the young. The Department of Public Welfare supervises numerous institutions for juveniles and has developed special programs for delinquent children. (See section on Youth Institutions in chapter 11.)

The Juvenile Court Judges Commission sets standards, develops procedures, advises Juvenile Court judges in the proper methods of dealing with the young in the courts, and administers juvenile probation programs. The commission is made up of nine judges serving three-year terms. The governor appoints the members from a list of Common Pleas judges submitted by the chief justice of the Supreme Court.

Probation and Parole

The Pennsylvania Board of Probation and Parole provides the Commonwealth with a single, coordinated parole system. The board is an independent administrative agency consisting of five members appointed by the governor with Senate consent. Authorized to parole and reparole, commit and recommit for violations of parole, and to discharge from parole, the board also has some supervisory authority over persons on probation. It collects and maintains records of all persons on probation or parole and supervises parolees from other states residing in Pennsylvania. The board assists parolees in finding employment after release from prison. Before a decision on parole is made, Pennsylvania law requires that the conduct of persons in prison and their backgrounds be investigated, including the circumstances that led to the offenses committed. The Board of Probation and Parole makes recommendations to the Board of Pardons.

Board of Pardons

The Board of Pardons hears pleas for pardons and commutations of sentences and submits recommendations to the governor. The board is made up of the lieutenant governor, who is chairperson, the attorney general, a penologist, an attorney, and either a doctor or a psychiatrist. The Board of Pardons holds public hearings in Philadelphia, Harrisburg, and Pittsburgh.

For further information on topics in this chapter, see the following sources in *Key to Further Information:*

Administrator of Pennsylvania Courts

Pennsylvania Bar Association

5

Financing Government

Pennsylvania assumes the responsibility for a complex array of services for the welfare of its citizens. Through the collection of taxes, licenses, and other fees and the sale of lottery tickets, the state directly funds education, health, economic development, income maintenance, transportation, social development, protection of persons and property, and recreation programs.

The state budget is a plan for the collection and disbursement of public monies for a given year. Because it reflects spending priorities, the budget is also an outline of proposed government activities. Article VIII, Section 12(a) of the state constitution states that the governor must submit annually to the General Assembly:

> . . . a balanced operating budget for the ensuing fiscal year setting forth in detail (1) proposed expenditures classified by department

The Budget

or agency and by program and (2) estimated revenue from all sources.

Pennsylvania's fiscal year begins on July 1 and ends on June 30 of the following year. Pennsylvania has no procedure for continuing the funding of state supported programs after the end of the fiscal year; therefore the budget bill must be passed and signed by June 30.

The governor is also required to submit a capital budget, financed through general revenue bonds and a five-year fiscal plan for the Commonwealth. The legislature is not required to act on capital budgets every year.

Budget Process

The governor's budget secretary works with budget analysts, department financial experts, and

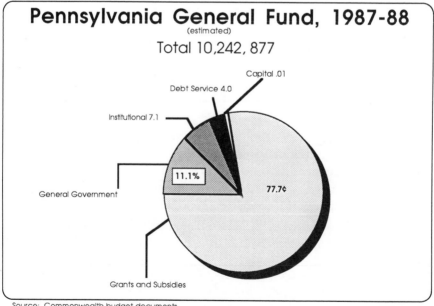

Pennsylvania General Fund, 1987-88
(estimated)

Total 10,242,877

Capital .01

Debt Service 4.0

Institutional 7.1

11.1%

77.7¢

General Government

Grants and Subsidies

Source: Commonwealth budget documents

heads of departments, boards, commissions, and other agencies to prepare the budget to be submitted to the legislature. Requests are developed and transmitted on an on-line computer system. Conferences between the budget secretary and agencies are held for the purpose of arriving at a better understanding of spending requirements. By law, the budget secretary must present recommendations to the governor prior to January 1 and the governor must submit the budget to the General Assembly "as soon as possible," usually in February or March. The Appropriations Committees of both houses then hold hearings, providing an opportunity for agency personnel to defend and justify their requests to the legislators.

A general appropriation bill covers funds for the executive, legislative, and judicial branches of government and for public debt service and the public schools. All other appropriations are made indi-

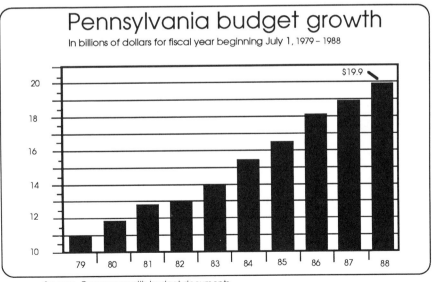

Pennsylvania budget growth

In billions of dollars for fiscal year beginning July 1, 1979 – 1988

$19.9

Source: Commonwealth budget documents

vidually by separate special bills. Nonpreferred appropriation bills, which require a two-thirds vote of both houses, are for state-related universities and other institutions not under the absolute control of the Commonwealth. The governor has the power to reduce or item veto an appropriation considered excessive or unnecessary.

Commonwealth Indebtedness

Article VIII, Section 7.1 of the state constitution allows the Commonwealth to incur debts under certain circumstances. The limit of state borrowing is set by the constitution at 1.75 times the average yearly tax collections over a period of five years. Excluded from the debt limits are debts approved by voter referendum, providing the debt is for a purpose specifically itemized in the law authorizing the debt. Debt that is self-liquidating from sources other than Commonwealth revenues or debt, such as that incurred by authorities, is not considered Commonwealth indebtedness. Any debt incurred for capital projects must be amortized over a period of time not to exceed the useful life of such projects. The constitution requires the State Treasurer to set aside funds to pay principal and interest on the state debt in the event that insufficient funds are appropriated by the legislature.

Audits

The state constitution requires financial auditing of the Commonwealth and all its affiliates. The Auditor General performs the financial post audit; the Office of Budget conducts the performance audit on selected programs.

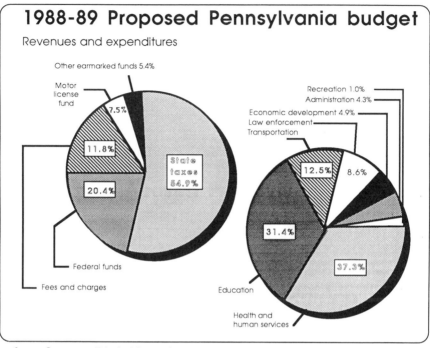

1988-89 Proposed Pennsylvania budget

Revenues and expenditures

Other earmarked funds 5.4%

Motor license fund 7.5%

11.8%

20.4%

State taxes 54.9%

Federal funds

Fees and charges

Recreation 1.0%
Administration 4.3%
Economic development 4.9%
Law enforcement
Transportation

12.5%   8.6%

31.4%

37.3%

Education

Health and human services

Source: Commonwealth budget documents

Taxes and Revenue

The general fund is the major operating fund of the Commonwealth. All tax receipts and other types of revenue not specified by law as belonging in special funds are deposited in the general fund. Except for certain restricted receipts, general fund income is appropriated in specific amounts to meet the budgetary requirements of governmental programs.

The major sources of general-fund revenue are corporation taxes, sales tax, and personal income tax. The estimated general-fund revenue for the 1987–88 fiscal year is $10.2 billion. Over one-half the general-fund budget went for elementary, secondary, and higher education support.

Personal Income Tax

The flat-rate income tax passed in 1971, designed to conform to the uniformity clause of the state constitution, allows no deductions and provides no graduated rates. The uniformity clause Article VIII, Section 1 reads:

> All taxes shall be uniform, upon the same class of subjects, within the territorial limits of the authority levying the tax, and shall be levied and collected under general laws.

The tax is levied against taxable income of resident and nonresident individuals, estates, and trusts. There is a poverty exemption and a deduction is permitted for certain unreimbursed business expenses. Persons over fifty-five years of age can have a one-time exclusion of the gain from the sale of a principal residence.

Consumption Taxes

A variety of taxes on goods and services provide 40 percent of the general fund.

Statutes require that proceeds from the sales, use, and hotel-occupancy tax be applied to education. The sales tax is collected on specific goods and services sold at retail. Significant exceptions are food, beverages, wearing apparel, and drugs. The use tax is collected on goods and services upon which tax has not been paid, generally those purchased outside that state and used in Pennsylvania. The hotel-occupancy tax is imposed on rooms rented for less than thirty days. These taxes represent approximately one-third of the revenue for the general fund for 1987–88.

Other consumption taxes include assessments on cigarettes, liquor, and malt beverages.

Corporate Taxes

The Corporate Net Income Tax (CNI) originated as an emergency tax during the Civil War. It was later declared unconstitutional and was not used again until revenue emergencies in 1923 and 1935. The CNI was made permanent in 1957 through constitutional amendment and became part of the Tax Reform Code of 1971.

Businesses are also subject to corporate loans, capital stock, and franchise taxes. Common carriers pay a tax on gross receipts. The Public Utility Realty Tax is levied against certain utility services regulated by the Public Utility Commission in lieu of a local real-property tax. Banks and other financial institutions are taxed on the value of their stock.

Pennsylvania's overall tax structure is comparable to other states. Corporate taxes make up about 24 percent of the general-fund budget. There has been no increase in corporate taxes since 1979 and the corporate net income tax, after having reached a high of 12 percent in 1972, decreased to 8.5 percent in 1987.

A job-creation tax credit is given to employers who hire persons who are subject to federal unemployment compensation.

Revenue Funds

Certain state revenues are earmarked for specific purposes. There are ninety-four funds into which revenue is placed. Of these, three funds (the general, the motor license, and the lottery) contain the principal part of state revenue. General-fund revenues are available for appropriation by the General Assembly for any statutory purpose. Motor License Fund revenues are used solely for highway programs, bridges, and air navigation facilities. This revenue can be used for construction, reconstruction, maintenance, repairs, and for the payment of debts incurred for these purposes. The Motor License Fund also finances state police operations. Lottery Fund revenues are specified for programs benefiting senior citizens.

When persons or businesses sell or purchase property, a realty-transfer tax of 1 percent of actual price of the property must be paid. Tax stamps or meter impressions, indicating payment of the tax, are affixed to the document by the county Recorder of Deeds.

Pennsylvania began lottery sales in 1972 with the specific purpose of funding programs that benefit senior citizens. (See chapter 11, Human Services.)

Other examples of special revenue funds are the game, fish, boating, banking department, milk marketing, state harness racing, state horse racing, and the catastrophic-loss funds.

Local Revenues

Local governments in Pennsylvania receive their taxing authority from the state legislature, which prescribes the tax base and tax limitations for each class of government. Local taxes are imposed by many different jurisdictions, some overlapping, each differing to some extent in powers and classification. These jurisdictions are counties, cities, boroughs, townships, towns, school districts, and institution districts. Home-rule municipalities may set their own rates of taxation for property and for various other taxes on residents, but they are bound by state laws governing taxes and assessments.

All taxing authorities are permitted to levy taxes on real estate, although the maximum millage permitted varies. Counties may levy a four mill personal property tax. Local governments may impose a variety of special-purpose taxes. These vary from one class of government to another, and their purpose ranges from providing pension funds, street lighting, erecting a municipal building, to supporting library services. Some special-purpose taxes may be enacted by action of the governing body, some only with the consent of the voters, and others only by court order.

Act 511 of 1965, the Local Tax Enabling Act, permits, with a few exceptions, local taxing of any subject not already taxed by the state. Act 511 applies to all political subdivisions except counties, the city of Philadelphia, and the school district of Philadelphia. Taxes most commonly levied under this act are earned income, per capita, flat-rate occupation, assessed occupation or occupational privilege, real estate transfer, amusement, and the mercantile or gross-receipts tax (a tax on the gross receipts from the sale of goods, wares, and merchandise by retail and wholesale dealers). Similar but more extensive taxing powers are conveyed to Philadelphia by the Sterling Act of 1932.

Certain revenues are collected by the Commonwealth and returned to local governments. Part of the public-utility realty tax is returned to municipalities. Some liquid-fuels tax funds are returned to counties, cities, boroughs, and townships for roads and capital expenditures. Sales and use taxes go into the general fund for school districts.

Collection of State Taxes

Individual income taxes are collected by withholding from earnings and by direct payment. Sales and use taxes are collected from the buyer at the time of purchase and are then forwarded to the state. Most other taxes are collected at the source of the transaction.

The state Department of Revenue administers the collection of all state taxes and receives all monies due the Commonwealth. Various bureaus of the department administer taxes relating to personal income, corporations, cigarettes, and beverages. The sales and use tax and those taxes collected by a county, such as inheritance, realty, fishing, and hunting, are also collected separately. Local governments collect their own taxes and finance this collection without state subsidy.

Assessment Procedures

All assessments of real property are required by law to be made "according to actual value." The assessment laws state that, in determining such value, the sale price, estimated or actual, shall be considered but shall not be a controlling element. Real-property assessments in fourth- through eighth-class counties are based upon an established predetermined ratio not exceeding 75 percent of actual value. Roughly 19 percent of real property in the state, with a value of approximately $37.6 billion, is tax-exempt.

Specific subjects of and exemptions from real-property taxation are enumerated in various assessment laws and in the state constitution. For example, a 1973 constitutional amendment permits reduced assessments for certain agricultural and forest lands. Owners of ten acres of farmland, agricultural reserves, or forest preserves can apply for a reduced assessment based on use value rather than market value. Farmers with ten acres or less of land may receive a preferential assessment if they have farmed the land for the preceding three years and can show that they anticipate a yearly gross income of $2,000 or more from the land. If the land changes use, the landowner must pay a "rollback" in the amount of the tax reduction received (for a period of up to seven years) plus 6 percent interest on the rollback. Act 515 is a similar law that permits all counties to grant use value assessments.

Consolidation and standardization of present assessment laws have been of concern to the General Assembly. Proposals to make procedures uniform and to provide for statewide supervision and enforcement to equalize assessments have been under consideration. At present, the State Tax Equalization Board (see chapter 2, The Executive) has the responsibility for determining annually the market value of taxable property in each political subdivision and school district in the state. The board does not have the power to change or in any way control assessments of property as established by county and local taxing authorities. The market values it determines, however, are used as a factor for distribution of state subsidies to school districts, state aid to libraries, and for various other purposes in state and local government. The board establishes a common-level ratio for each county for the previous calendar year.

Special Tax Exemptions

Property-tax rebates and income-tax credits are available for some low-income residents in Allegheny and Philadelphia counties and for all Pennsylvania home-owner veterans who are 100 percent disabled. Low-income senior citizens can qualify for a tax rebate from state lottery funds, and a taxpayer who meets poverty income standards is eligible for full or partial exemptions from the Pennsylvania income tax.

Businesses who construct new plants or expand their businesses may be eligible for abatement of local real estate taxes for up to ten years.

Federal Participation

Federal funds received by Pennsylvanians amounted to approximately $3.9 billion in 1987. The Federal Omnibus Budget Reconciliation Act of 1981 established block grants to the state for eight specific programs, plus special funding for job training under the Job Training Partnership Act. Block grants are received to fund the following: community services (90 percent going to Community Action Agencies programs); small communities for community development projects, education, maternal and child care, preventive health care and health services, drug and alcohol and mental health, social services; and the Low Income Home Energy Assistance Program.

For further information on topics in this chapter, see the following sources in *Key to Further Information:*

Commonwealth of Pennsylvania Executive Budget

Pennsylvania Economy League

6

Local Government

Pennsylvanians are residents not only of the Commonwealth but also of a county, a school district, and a city, borough, or township in which they live. Pennsylvania has 67 counties, 54 cities, 967 boroughs, one incorporated town, 1,550 townships (91 first class; 1,459 second class), and 501 school districts. The number and variety of local governments in Pennsylvania are exceeded only by those in the state of Illinois.

The powers and responsibilities of local governments are defined by the Pennsylvania Constitution and by statutes passed by the General Assembly. Each class of municipality operates under a legal code that defines its governmental structure and its general and specific powers. Each unit of local government is distinct, although counties and school districts may encompass more than one municipality. The separate units may cooperate with each other to serve the public.

Governmental Units

The General Assembly has classified counties, cities, and townships on the basis of population. A change in the classification of a county or city is justified by the results of the two preceding United States censuses. Changes in classifications are relatively rare and are not made on the basis of a temporary fluctuation in population.

Counties

The number of counties in Pennsylvania has remained constant since 1878. Nine classes of counties range from counties of the first class with a population of at least 1,500,000 to counties of the eighth class with less than 20,000 population. (Note: Two types of second-class counties, "second class" and "second class A," account for the total of nine classes.)

Philadelphia, a consolidated city-county, is the sole first-class county; Allegheny is the only second-class county; Montgomery and Delaware are both second-class A counties. The remaining sixty-three counties are distributed among the remaining six classes.

Since the eighteenth century the role of the county in Pennsylvania had been primarily as an agent of the state for administering justice, keeping legal records, conducting elections, and administering some social welfare programs. Recent legislation has increased the policy-making powers of the county commissioners to include such areas as urban development, regional planning, community colleges, county health programs, and limited zoning regulations. Additional functions include the assessment of property for local tax purposes and the construction and maintenance of county buildings and other public facilities. In general,

though, counties have limited powers and responsibilities, and their officials have limited discre-
tion in the conduct of local affairs.

Counties that have not adopted a home-rule
charter are governed by a board of three county
commissioners elected every four years. In the primary election each political party nominates two
candidates for county commissioner, thus ensuring that at least one of the three elected is a member of a minority party.

Although the law allows consolidation of some
offices in smaller counties, the constitution speci-
fies that counties elect the following officials in
addition to three commissioners: sheriff, prothonotary, register of wills, recorder of deeds, clerk of
courts, district attorney, treasurer, and controller
or three auditors. These officials are, to a large
extent, independent of the county commissioners.
Their powers and duties are prescribed by statutes
in the county codes and in general state law.

Cities

Pennsylvania has four classes of cities. These municipal governments have broad responsibilities to
make administrative and policy decisions, levy
taxes, borrow money, and authorize expenditures.

Philadelphia, with a population of more than a
million and a half, is the only city designated as
first class. Pittsburgh is designated as second
class and Scranton as second class A. The fifty
third-class cities in Pennsylvania all have populations under 135,000. The smallest city, Parker
City, is designated as unclassified.

Philadelphia, the oldest and largest city in Pennsylvania, has had a home-rule charter since 1951.
The elected mayor is assisted by a managing direc-

tor who supervises ten major departments, and by a director of finance, a city solicitor, and a city representative, all of whom are appointed. The city council of seventeen has seven members elected at large and ten elected as representatives of each of the ten councilmanic districts of the city. Each political party nominates one candidate for each of the ten district positions and five candidates for the seven at-large positions, thereby ensuring at least two council members from a minority party.

Pittsburgh and Scranton, second-class and second-class A cities, respectively, adopted home-rule charters in 1974. Their mayors, like the mayor of Philadelphia, have wide appointive and removal powers, can recommend measures to the council, and may veto legislation passed by the council. A two-thirds majority of the council is required to override the veto.

In third-class cities, the mandated form of government is the commission, but from 1957 to 1972 the cities in this category were allowed, through voter referendum, to modify their local charters by replacing the commission with either a strong mayor-council or council-manager form of government. Sixteen cities now operate under such optional charters. Since 1972, third-class cities must follow procedures in Act 62 to change their form of government.

Under the commission form of city government, the mayor, acting as president, and four other members constitute the commission. Each commission member is responsible for one of the five major departments of the city: public affairs (always headed by the mayor), accounts and finance, public safety, streets and public improvements, and parks and public property. Along with the controller and treasurer, these officials are elected at large for four-year overlapping terms. The council appoints other staff, including the city clerk, city engineer, and city solicitor, all of whom also serve for four years.

In the mayor-council form of government, the council may have five, seven, or nine members elected at large for staggered four-year terms. The mayor, treasurer, and controller are also elected for four years. The mayor, as chief executive of the city, has no vote in the council but possesses a veto that two-thirds of the council can override. The mayor enforces council decisions, supervises the work of all city departments, and submits the annual budget to the council for its approval.

Under the council-manager form of government, all power is vested in the council. The council may be made up of five, seven, or nine members elected at large for four-year terms. The council elects one of its own members as mayor who presides over meetings, and who may vote on matters before the council but lacks veto power. A city clerk and city manager are appointed by the council. The manager, who is the chief administrative officer of the city, carries out the ordinances of the council, makes recommendations to the council, prepares and executes an annual budget, and usually appoints and removes department heads and other administrative personnel. The manager has no vote in council meetings.

Boroughs

The present type of borough government was characteristic of municipalities in the nineteenth century. Most present cities were boroughs first and became cities as their populations increased.

The mandated form of government for boroughs is known as the "weak mayor" form, although boroughs may exercise the option of adopting an ordinance for a council-manager form. Without a manager, boroughs have no single administrative head. The mayor is not a member of the council and can only vote on a matter before council to break a tie. Council members are elected for four-year overlapping terms; the mayor is also elected for four years. Boroughs that are divided into wards have at least one, and not more than two, council members, who are elected from each ward. In boroughs not divided into wards, seven council members are elected at-large.

Council decisions are framed in the form of ordinances and resolutions that must be passed by the majority of members voting and signed by the mayor. A majority in council can override a veto by the mayor. The council's powers are extensive, covering the whole range of municipal functions. In boroughs with managers, the council-appointed manager undertakes these administrative duties sometimes with committee help. When there is no manager, council members often work in committees to direct borough activities.

Since boroughs have no specific population requirement, they are not classified. The population of the 967 boroughs ranges from 16 residents to 36,000. Nine boroughs have fewer than 100 residents and 379 have fewer than 1,000. Forty-nine boroughs have a population of more than 10,000.

Townships

Townships in Pennsylvania are divided into two classes. All townships not designated as first class are considered second class townships. First-class townships require a population density of at least 300 persons per square mile, but many townships that meet that density requirement have remained second-class townships. Voters must approve the change to a first-class township in a referendum.

First-class townships have a commission form of government, electing from five to fifteen commissioners with four-year overlapping terms. The commissioners are empowered to appoint a manager.

In second-class townships, three supervisors are elected for six-year staggered terms. If approved by the voters in a referendum, two additional supervisors may be elected. The board of supervisors is the administrative and legislative body of the township. Second-class townships may also appoint a manager.

A borough or township that exceeds 10,000 population may be chartered as a third-class city.

School Districts

Boards of school directors are the governing agencies for local school districts with full power to carry out the responsibilities assigned by law. They may levy taxes (except in Philadelphia, where city council is the taxing authority), issue bonds, hire personnel, provide for school buildings, and purchase textbooks and supplies. School districts are divided into five classifications according to population and, with the exception of Philadelphia, are administered by nine-member school boards elected either at-large or by regions for four-year overlapping terms. In Philadelphia, the mayor appoints the nine-member school board for staggered four-year terms from a list submitted by a nonpartisan nominating panel. The superintendent is the administrative head of the local school district.

Changing Local Government: Home Rule and Optional Plans

The United States Constitution does not mention local government, and so control over municipalities is reserved to the states. This power over local governments has been closely guarded by state legislatures so that municipalities could do little without specific authorization from the state legislature. This one-sided relationship is known as Dillon's rule: "Municipal corporations owe their origins to, and derive their powers and rights wholly from, the legislature. . . ."

The 1967–68 Constitutional Convention recognized the need for more efficiency in local government and so rewrote Article IX, the local government article, and empowered the legislature to implement the plan. In April 1972 the General Assembly passed Act 62, the Home Rule Charter and Optional Plans Law. Home rule for municipalities was designed to change the nature of the historic relationship between communities and the state resulting from Dillon's rule. Home rule enables local municipalities and counties to determine their own structures of government and the services they will perform.

Act 62, which applies to counties, cities, boroughs, and townships, allows the voters in a specific municipality or county to elect a government study commission to study their present government structure and to consider alternate forms available under this law. The commission may recommend a home-rule charter or an optional form of government. How the ballot is worded limits the scope of the study commission. The government study commission may also recommend that no change is needed. A proposal by the study commission for home rule or an optional plan must be accepted or rejected by the voters in a referendum and, if approved, would go into effect at the next municipal election following such approval.

Candidates for government study commissions

do not run as party members but must file nomination papers as independent candidates. All voters, regardless of how they are registered, may vote for these candidates in either the spring or fall election.

After the passage of Act 62, home-rule charters were proposed in many communities in the state. Between 1972 and 1976, forty-nine municipalities adopted home rule. Since 1976, only eight additional municipalities have opted for home rule.

Home-Rule Charter

A home-rule charter is a written document setting forth the form, powers, and duties of the government, that must include an elected, representative governing body. A charter can only be adopted, amended, or repealed by vote of the citizens of the governmental unit. Those municipalities and counties adopting home rule are then no longer subject to the state codes for that class of government.

Home rule gives communities a broader range of power than they have traditionally possessed. Local governments with home rule may exercise any powers not denied to them, the reverse of the established pattern in which they can exercise only those powers permitted them. In adopting home rule, municipalities and counties can change their form of government or keep the existing one.

The fifty-nine communities that have adopted home-rule charters include five counties: Delaware, Erie, Lackawanna, Lehigh, and Northampton; twelve cities, including Philadelphia; twenty-five townships; and seventeen boroughs. Of the eleven communities that have adopted optional plans, there are six townships, three cities, and two boroughs.

A home-rule charter may be written to allow people in a given municipality or county to bring about change through initiative by putting a referendum on the local ballot. The Pennsylvania Constitution has no provision for similar action on the state level.

Optional Plans of Government

A city, borough, township, or county that elects a plan from among the optional forms possible under Act 62 is able to exercise only those powers specifically granted to it, chiefly through its municipal class code. While not gaining any new power, municipalities selecting an optional plan achieve structural and administrative change necessary for effective government.

Act 62 offers six alternative plans to municipalities: three variations of an executive or mayor-council plan, a council-manager plan, a plan limited to counties to select from those four plans, and a small-municipality plan, limited to any municipality having a population of fewer than 7,500.

Within each of these plans, additional options are possible so that a newly formed government may be tailored to meet the needs of a specific municipality. The elected government study commission that recommends an optional form of government includes in its report recommendations on the size of the council and the basis on which it is to be elected, whether by district, at large, or a combination of both.

Authorities   Authorities, first established in 1933, were originally created to avoid the unrealistic debt limits imposed by the Pennsylvania Constitution prior to the 1968 revision. Their number has risen dramatically as units of local government and school districts have chosen this means of acquiring, constructing, maintaining, and operating all sorts of public facilities, including airports, schools, highways, parkways, hospitals, and industrial and commercial development projects. Authorities continue to be used for their management and jurisdictional advantages, particularly in the case of multiple municipalities. There are currently more than 2,500 authorities in Pennsylvania.

The money borrowed to construct and operate municipal authority projects is not considered municipal debt, limited by the constitution and the Local Government Unit Debt Act. This act sets limits on the amount of money a county, local municipality, or school district may borrow unless that debt is supported by user fees as determined by the Department of Community Affairs. If the project is leased back to the municipality, lease-rental debt counts against the municipal debt limit.

An authority is a special kind of local unit. It is not a general governmental unit like a city, borough, or township. An authority is established by ordinance passed by one or more county, city, town, borough, township, or school district of the Commonwealth acting singly or jointly with any other municipality.

The governing body of a municipality or school district appoints the members of an authority board, which, if appointed by one local government, consists of five members. If appointed by two or more municipalities (a joint municipal authority), at least one member is appointed from each area.

An authority acts as a financing instrument, issuing bonds to pay for the initial cost of a project. Costs, including construction, acquisition, maintenance, and operation, must be met from bond issues, from rental revenues, or from other revenues earned by the project. An authority cannot levy taxes, and tax money cannot be spent directly for authority purposes, although a municipality or school district can use tax revenue to pay authority rental charges.

Once a project is completed, a municipality or school district may choose to have the authority operate the facility, or the municipality may assume the operation and management for itself and pay rent to the authority (the lease-back authority). The latter form is typical of local school-building authorities. The State Public School Building Authority, administered by the Department of Education, may be used as an adjunct to or in lieu of local school-building authorities.

Cooperation Among Governmental Units

Article IX, Section 5 of the Constitution of 1968 provides that a municipality, by act of its governing body or by initiative and referendum in the area affected, may cooperate with, delegate, or transfer functions to any other governmental unit, including a school district, the federal government, or another state. The Municipalities Planning Code encourages joint planning as well. Cooperative arrangements occur today between and among all levels and types of governments.

Boundary Change

The Pennsylvania Supreme Court has held that because the General Assembly has failed to enact uniform boundary-change legislation, the only way that municipalities can be merged, consolidated, or have their boundaries changed is through voter initiative and referendum.

Council of Governments

A popular form of cooperation is a Council of Governments (COG). A COG is a voluntary association of local government units joined together under a written compact as a device to improve cooperation, coordination, and planning. Currently 50 councils of governments, encompassing more than 250 municipalities, operate in the state. A COG provides a means for local officials to work together and to coordinate programs and projects for maximum efficiency, economy, and community well-being. Financing is derived from voluntary annual dues paid by member municipalities, state and federal grants, and grants from other public and private agencies. Typical COG services include cooperative purchasing, environmental control, health planning, housing codes, law enforcement, library services, recreation, refuse collection, transportation, water-quality management, federal grant management, and sometimes tax collection.

State Assistance to Local Governments

It is difficult to designate many services as strictly local because of overlapping local, state, and federal government responsibilities. For example, housing programs receive large federal grants. State and federal grants and loans are available for sewage disposal facilities. Local police are assisted by the state police and the Federal Bureau of Investigation. Local services such as libraries, parks, recreation, and planning are usually state and federally funded to some degree. Education is considered a local function, yet state funds account for approximately one-half of the total revenue of local public schools.

Department of Community Affairs

The Department of Community Affairs was established in 1966 to provide a system of services and programs to foster the development of Pennsylvania's communities. Departmental activities are carried out through technical assistance and funding for housing, redevelopment, planning, recreation, economic development, flood-plain management, employment training and related services, and for dealing with municipal fiscal distress. Act 47, the distressed communities law administered by the DCA, provides relief for municipalities facing the danger of bankruptcy. The department encourages regional planning and development and researches problems that affect local affairs. DCA administers the flood-plain-management program, which requires that flood-prone municipalities develop ordinances to restrict building in the flood plain.

DCA provides a consulting service and training program for local governments that includes all phases of municipal operations and keeps municipal statistics and records. It provides technical assistance to regional, county, and municipal planning agencies and also administers the state planning assistance program that grants state funds to municipal and regional planning groups.

The state provides additional services to local governments through the Departments of Commerce, Environmental Resources, Health, Transportation, Labor and Industry, and Welfare. Local school districts receive services from the Department of Education.

Citizen Participation

The Pennsylvania Sunshine Law mandates that all meetings held by a board, council, commission, or committee of any political subdivision must be open to the public. This provides citizens the opportunity to observe the deliberations of their local government bodies. Adequate notice of open meetings must be provided. The same exceptions apply as on the state level and include executive sessions held to discuss employment, strategy for collective bargaining or litigation, real estate contracts, and certain other specific matters. The only enforcement is through citizen action.

For further information on topics in this chapter, see the following sources in *Key to Further Information:*

A Citizen's Guide to Pennsylvania Local Government

Pennsylvania Economy League

Pennsylvania Statistical Abstract

7

Elections and Political Parties

Every citizen's right to vote is protected by the Constitution of the United States. No state may set voting qualifications that discriminate on the basis of race, color, or sex. All citizens are guaranteed equal protection under the federal Constitution.

Voters

Traditionally, states have had the power to set voter qualifications. The Fifteenth and Nineteenth Amendments to the Constitution, however, provide that states may not deny citizens the right to vote on account of race, color, or sex. The Twenty-fourth Amendment prohibits a poll tax. In addition to the constitutional limits on state power, federal law prohibits states from requiring persons to pass literacy tests in order to register or vote.

The Voting Rights Act of 1965, amended by Congress in 1970, 1975, and again in 1986, protects and strengthens the right of all citizens to vote in the United States. The purpose of the Voting

Voting Rights Act

Rights Act is to ensure that no citizen is denied the right to vote because of discrimination due to race or language.

The Voting Rights Act requires all states to permit absentee registration and voting for president and vice president, and sets residence requirements (thirty days before the election) for voting in presidential elections. Qualified voters who have moved within thirty days of a presidential election must be allowed to vote in person or by absentee ballot at their former place of residence.

In 1975 Congress amended the Voting Rights Act to require states, counties, and towns with significant numbers of Spanish-speaking persons, American Indians, or Alaskan natives to conduct elections in the language of the minority group as well as in English. Although the law is complex, the intent is clear: racial and language-minority citizens should have the same rights and opportunities as other Americans to participate in politics and government.

The Voting Rights Act also does the following:

- Sets penalties, including fines and imprisonment for public officials or private individuals who deny citizens the right to vote
- Permits citizens whose voting rights have been violated to go to court to request federal intervention to protect those rights (such intervention is clearly spelled out in the act)
- Permits the winning side in a voting rights lawsuit to recover the attorney's fees from the government that is involved and whose public officials have failed to protect the citizen's voting rights
- Provides that federal examiners can be appointed to draw up a list of eligible voters for

local election officials when some indication of discriminatory registration exists

- Provides that federal observers can be appointed as poll watchers at local polling places to ensure that all eligible voters are allowed to vote and that all ballots are accurately counted

Voting in Pennsylvania

In order to qualify as a voter in Pennsylvania an individual must be at least eighteen years of age (by the day after the election), a citizen of the United States for at least one month, a resident of the state and election district thirty days immediately preceding the election or primary, and must be registered to vote.

In Pennsylvania mental patients are eligible to vote, as are those persons in penal institutions awaiting trial or who have been convicted of certain misdemeanors. Only incarcerated felons cannot vote.

Individuals qualified to vote in a primary, general, or municipal election may register during the regular registration period preceding that election. They may register in person at the county board of elections or by mail, using mail-registration forms available at election boards, post offices, party committees, state stores, banks, libraries, or from the League of Women Voters. Registration offices are often found in county courthouses.

Citizens can register at any time except for thirty days before and after the November election, and thirty days before and five days after the primary. Party enrollment may be changed throughout the year during open registration in person or by mail.

At the time of registration individuals can specify a party affiliation. Voters with no party affiliation cannot vote for candidates in primary elections but can vote on ballot questions. Candidates from minor political parties usually are not on the primary ballot.

Registration is permanent unless a voter fails to vote for two years. In that case the county board of elections must send a notice that registration will be cancelled unless reinstatement is requested by the voter within thirty days. The voter may sign and return the card to be reinstated.

Voters who change their residence or name must reregister unless they reside in the same county, in which case they need only fill out a change-of-address card or change-of-name card in person or by mail. Once registered, a voter's registration card with a serial number and the signature of the registrar is placed in the district register. Cards of those voters who need assistance in voting because of physical disability or illiteracy must specify the reason.

Absentee Registration

The federal Voting Rights Act provides for absentee registration for all citizens living abroad for presidential and vice-presidential elections only.

Absentee registration for state and local elections is permitted for Pennsylvania citizens in government or military service, employed overseas, or serving with religious or welfare groups outside the state. Absentee registration is also available for their spouses and dependents. Military or government personnel are registered in the district where they resided immediately prior to entering such service.

Machine Voting

At a primary, before voters are admitted to a booth in a district using voting machines, the election officer in charge adjusts the machine so that voters can vote only for the candidates of the party in which they are registered. They then vote for candidates individually by operating the lever adjacent to each candidate's name.

At municipal and general elections voters wishing to vote a straight party ticket may do so by operating the single political-party lever if the machine is so equipped. In all other instances voters operate the levers next to the names of the candidates of their choice.

When voting by machine, voters do not invalidate their vote when they turn an incorrect lever by accident. If they make a mistake or change their minds, they need only put the lever back to its original position and turn the proper lever.

Space is provided on all voting machines for write-in votes. To vote for a person whose name does not appear on the ballot, a voter opens the slot which is either at the top of or to the left of the office listing. The write-in slot should not be opened unless the voter intends to use it because once the slot is open, the lever for that office is locked. If a voter can vote for several candidates for a particular office (school directors, for example), the voter may use the write-in slot for one (or more) and pull the levers for the remainder, as long as the total does not exceed the number of votes permitted for that office. A voter can write in the candidate's name or place a sticker in the opening.

After voting, a voter either pushes a red button or operates a large handle, depending on the type of machine. This both records the individual's vote and opens the curtain.

Electronic Voting

Since the 1980 passage of a law authorizing the use of electronic voting systems, several different systems have been approved for use in Pennsylvania. In order to adopt an electronic voting system for use, voters of the county or municipality must authorize such use. Presently twenty-five counties use electronic voting systems. To vote for a person whose name does not appear as a candidate (write-in), the elector shall ask an election official for instructions.

Electronic voting systems permit voters to record their votes manually, electronically, or through some combination thereof, and then the votes are automatically tabulated by machine. As voting machines age, and paper-ballot districts consider change, additional counties may adopt electronic voting systems.

Ballot Voting

Voters voting by paper ballot make a cross (X) or check ($\sqrt{}$) in the square to the right of the name of the candidate for whom they wish to vote. Those wishing to vote for a person whose name is not on the ballot may write, print, or paste the name in the blank space provided for that purpose; they must use only black lead pencil, or a pen with blue or black ink. All markings placed on the ballot must be made by the same pencil or pen and must be all crosses (x) or all checks ($\sqrt{}$).

The election code provides that the election officer in charge of ballots detaches one at a time, folds the ballot so that only the back is visible, and then hands it to the voter. When the ballot is received, the voter goes into a polling booth, draws the curtain, marks the ballot, and before leaving the booth, refolds the ballot. After leaving the booth, the voter shows the ballot to an election official, who checks the number to be certain it is the same ballot originally given the voter. The voter then removes the perforated corner containing the number and deposits the folded ballot in the ballot box.

At the current time paper ballots are used in a part or all of twenty-one counties, but this accounts for less than seven percent of the voting districts.

Absentee Voting

Pennsylvania provides for absentee voting for the following persons: members of the armed forces; voters who expect to be absent because of duties, occupation, or business (including vacations and leaves of absence); accompanying spouses and dependents of all the above; county employees who cannot vote because of duties on election day relating to the conduct of the election; those who will not attend a polling place because of religious observance; and those unable to get to the polls because of illness or physical disability. Voters with a permanent disability may be placed on a permanent absentee-ballot list by filing a physician's certificate of permanent disability. To remain on this list, the voter must submit a written statement of continuing disability to the county board of elections every four years.

Request for an application for an absentee ballot may be made in person, by mail, or by telephone.

The completed application must be received by the county board of elections no sooner than fifty days preceding the election or later than the Tuesday preceding the election. Ballots must be returned to the election board by 5 P.M. on the Friday before election. In presidential elections, ballots received between 5 P.M. Friday and the closing of the polls will be counted only for the presidential and vice-presidential offices.

Emergency application may be made until 5 P.M. on the Friday prior to the election. A voter who will be out of the county or hospitalized in the county on election day may both apply for an absentee ballot and cast the vote at the election board until that time. The ballot may be delivered by messenger if the voter is hospitalized.

Assistance in Voting

Assistance in voting is permitted if voters are unable to read or if a physical disability prevents them from operating the voting machine alone; this fact must be recorded on their registration card before election day. They must also swear or affirm that they need assistance and may select someone of their choice or may request a member of the board to assist them. The person must not be their employer or union steward.

All voters are entitled to receive instruction on how to operate the voting machine. The judge of elections may use a model or facsimile of the current sample ballot. However, no one may tell a voter for whom to vote.

Elections

Within the federal legal and judicial framework, each state enacts its own election laws, which vary in detail from one state to the next. In Pennsylvania the state constitution asserts that the right to secrecy in voting must be preserved, and the Election Code contains provisions directed toward this end. Pennsylvania law also establishes the requirements for registration and voting, nomination of candidates, and organization of the election process.

Elections are conducted, supervised, and controlled at three levels in Pennsylvania: (1) by the election board in each local election district (the geographical area in which all voters use the same polling place); (2) by the county board of elections, which consists of the county commissioners (in Philadelphia, the city commissioners) except in home-rule counties that do not have commissioners; and (3) by the Secretary of the Commonwealth and the Commissioner of Elections in the Department of State. For the election in which county commissioners are on the ballot, they are replaced on the board of elections by judges appointed by the president judge.

Types of Elections

Two elections are held each year in Pennsylvania: the primary and the general or municipal election. The primary is held on the third Tuesday of May except in presidential years, when it is held on the fourth Tuesday in April. The chief purpose of a primary is to nominate candidates who will be on the ballot in the fall election. Pennsylvania has a closed primary. This means that voters declare their party and vote only for candidates of that party. Only those registered in a political party may vote for candidates in a primary. Voters not registered in a political party may vote on ballot questions, for government study commission candidates, or in special elections if they are on a primary ballot. Special elections are sometimes held when a vacancy occurs in a local, state, or federal office. Ballot questions may include proposed constitutional amendments, bond elections, or other referenda.

Those elections held in even-numbered years are called general elections; municipal elections are held in odd-numbered years. Both take place on the first Tuesday after the first Monday in November and all registered voters may vote in them. School board elections are held at the same time and under the same rules as other elections.

Election Officials

The Secretary of the Commonwealth has many duties relative to elections. The secretary receives the results of elections, examines and approves types of voting systems, determines the form of nomination petitions, papers, and all other forms and records prescribed in the election code, certifies to county boards of elections the names of candidates for state and national offices, receives expense reports of all statewide candidates, and holds all returns and records for public inspection. The secretary also receives financial disclosure reports of statewide candidates.

County Boards of Elections

County boards of elections are required by law to publish in at least two newspapers of general circulation notices of elections, including offices to be filled, and the names of candidates for federal, state, county, and municipal offices. The board must also publish in full and explain the text of any constitutional amendments or ballot questions. This must be done no earlier than ten days, nor later than three days prior to the elections.

Sample ballots must be printed by the county board of elections and delivered to the polling places. On the Thursday preceding the primary the board is required to provide to any candidate requesting them, three specimen ballots or voting machine diagrams and one street list covering their political subdivision. On the Thursday preceding the November election the board must provide two specimen ballots or machine diagrams and ten copies of the street list to the county chairmen of all parties on the ballot. Parties and candidates may have more ballots printed at their own expense, but they must be of a different color.

Further duties of the county boards of elections include selecting and equipping polling places, making rules for the guidance of election officers, receiving nomination papers and petitions of candidates, and preparing registration totals before each election and submitting them to the Secretary of the Commonwealth. The boards also receive campaign financial reports from county and local candidates, investigate election fraud, report all suspicious circumstances to the district attorney, and pass on election results to the Secretary of the Commonwealth.

District Election Board

Pennsylvania is the only state that elects some members of each district election board. The district election board, which consists of a judge of election, a majority inspector, and a minority inspector, is responsible for the conduct of elections. Board members, who must be qualified registered voters in the district in which they serve, are elected for four-year terms. Each voter votes for one candidate as judge and one candidate as inspector. The person receiving the highest number of votes for judge receives that position. The individual with the highest number of votes for inspector becomes the majority inspector, while the person with the second highest number of votes becomes the minority inspector; both may be of the same political party. Each inspector appoints one clerk.

Local party chairs are sometimes asked to find a person to fill a vacancy on the board, or the position may be filled by appointment at a curbstone election—one that takes place on the morning of the election by requesting any voter of the district to serve in that position for the day.

Judge of Election

The judge of election is responsible for the conduct of the election and assigns specific duties to the election officers. The duties of the judge of election include supervising the custodial care of the voting register; receiving the keys to the voting machine, or in a paper ballot district, opening the packages of ballots; answering questions voters may have about how to use machines or ballots; keeping a record of voters who require assistance; examining and reading ballots or machine printouts and absentee ballots after the polls close; and returning the tally sheets, keys, ballots, and other materials to the county board of elections.

Inspectors of Election

Along with the judge, inspectors share responsibility for preparing the voting equipment before the polls open. One election officer handles the voters' certificates (signature cards); another compares voters' signatures in the district register and makes proper entries in it, and a third keeps a list of voters. Another clerk is responsible for the operation of the voting machine or receives and deposits ballots in the ballot box. The judge may rotate duties during the course of the day.

Constables

A constable, who is an officer of the court and not a member of the election board, may serve at the polling place as a peace officer and is assigned no other duties. If present, that person is paid at the same rate as the inspectors and clerks. Deputy constables can be appointed by the elected constable of a particular district. They must live in the municipality but not necessarily in the district in which they serve.

Overseers

On petition of five or more registered voters in any election district, the Court of Common Pleas must appoint two voters of that district, each of a different political party, as overseers to supervise the proceedings and to report to the court. They may be appointed as late as election day. Overseers may keep a list of voters, challenge any voters, and question them and their witnesses under oath about their right to vote. Overseers are required to sign the election returns of the district or to write on the returns the reason for their refusal to sign. They should report any fraud to the court immediately. Knowledge of fraudulent activity in a previous election or of such activity on the morning of election day can be cause to request overseers. Examples of fraudulent activity include voting by individuals not registered in the district, voting in the name of deceased persons, voting more than once by the same individuals, and illegal assistance to voters.

Watchers

In both a primary and general election, candidates are entitled to appoint two watchers in every election district where their names appear on the ballot. In a general or municipal election each political party and political body that has nominated candidates is entitled to appoint three watchers in every election district where its candidates appear on the ballot. All watchers must be qualified registered voters of the district in which they are authorized to watch. It is possible, however, for a watcher from another election district to be appointed on petition to the Court of Common Pleas.

Only one watcher per candidate at the primary or per political party or body at other elections can remain in the polling place at any one time prior to the closing of the polls. A watcher is permitted to keep a list of voters and is entitled to challenge any person making application to vote. At no time may watchers enter the enclosed space, defined as the area where the election officials perform their duties and voting takes place. It is legal for additional watchers, party committee members, campaigners, and candidates to remain near the polling place, but they must stay ten feet from the official polling room. After the polls close, all watchers may be in the polling place.

Challenges

Individuals are not entitled to vote at any election unless their registration cards appear in the district register and their signature compares with the voting register signature. Even though there is a card in the register, a voter may still be challenged by any qualified voter, election officer, overseer, or watcher as to identity, continued residence in the election district, or for other alleged violation.

Voters who are challenged as to identity or residence must produce at least one qualified voter from the election district as a witness to support their claim. Inspectors of election investigate and decide the qualifications of all persons claiming the right to vote. If they disagree, the judge of elections decides the question. If the judge of election is unable to decide, the overseers (if there are any) make the decision. If they cannot agree, the question is referred to the judge of the Court of Common Pleas, which sits in session on election day during the time the polls are open. Challenges to voters are rare.

After the polls close, the election officers record the number of votes cast in the manner prescribed by law.

Counting the Votes

Paper-Ballot Districts

In paper-ballot districts the election officers are responsible for counting the number of ballots cast and the number of voters who cast ballots. The officers must also seal the district register and package the voting checklist, unused ballots, and ballot stubs before the ballot box is opened.

Once the ballot box is opened, the judge or minority inspector reads aloud each ballot while the other observes. This must be done within the sight and hearing of the watchers and in the presence of the other election officials. The majority inspector and clerks record in ink on triplicate tally papers each vote as read. Persons handling the ballots may not have any pencil, pen, or stamp in their hands.

After all votes are counted, the officers must certify the number of votes cast for each person, the total number of ballots received, the number of votes cast, and the number of ballots declared void, cancelled, left blank, or spoiled. When the tally is complete, the following are deposited in the ballot box: the used ballots, including void, blank, and spoiled ballots; one tally paper; one numbered list of voters; and one oath of each election officer. The box is sealed, and the judge and minority inspector deliver it to the county board of elections together with the unused ballots. The minority inspector keeps a duplicate tally paper for one year. The remaining tally paper, numbered list of voters, and oaths of election officers are sealed in separate envelopes as soon as the count is completed. All envelopes are delivered by the judge of election to the county board of elections. Immediately after the vote has been counted, the election results are posted outside the polling place.

Ballots marked with any sign other than a cross (X) or check (√) are void. At the November election any erasure, mutilation, or defective marking of the straight party column renders the entire ballot void unless the voter has properly voted for candidates in single office, in which case the votes for such candidates are counted. Any erasure or mutilation in the vote for a single office voids the vote for that candidate but does not invalidate the rest of the ballot. If a write-in vote, stamp, or sticker is placed in the proper place, it will be counted. If a ballot is marked for more candidates than there are offices, or if it is impossible to determine who has been voted for, the vote for that office will not be counted. Ballots not marked, or improperly or defectively marked, are set aside but kept with the other ballots.

Machine Districts

After the polls close in voting-machine districts, the officers immediately lock and seal the operating lever of the machine. They note the number of votes cast as shown on the public counter and compare it with the number of voters shown on the numbered list of voters. The officers then remove the final print sheet with the vote totals from each machine. The judge and minority inspector, in view of the watchers and any others legally present, read off the totals for each office or question. The vote is recorded on the return sheets by the election officers and then signed. One of the tally sheets is posted outside the polling place. Remaining materials are returned to the county board of elections.

Electronic Systems Districts

Some electronic systems provide for central or regional tabulation of votes by the county board of elections, while other systems provide for election district tabulation. When done at the election district level, election officers must prepare duplicate records of the vote cast and post one outside the polling place. They also prepare general return sheets similar to those in paper-ballot and voting-machine districts. When tabulation is done at the county level, district election results must be posted in each election district no later than 5 P.M. of the second day following the election.

Counting Absentee Ballots

Absentee ballots are delivered to the appropriate election district by the county board of elections, and the names of persons to whom absentee ballots have been issued are posted at their local polling places. They are counted immediately after the polls close on election night. In electronic voting districts, the absentee ballots are counted along with other ballots from the election district at the location and in the manner specified by the county board of elections and provided for by the electronic voting system used.

Challenges may be made to absentee ballots on the grounds that the voter is not qualified in the district, or that the voter was in fact in the county during the time the polls were open, or that the absentee voter was physically able to appear at the polls. Such a challenge must be accompanied by a deposit of ten dollars, which will be refunded only if the challenge is sustained or withdrawn within five days. The deposit lessens the possibility of frivolous challenges.

Vote Recounts

If three qualified electors of an election district file a petition claiming fraud or error, a judge of the Court of Common Pleas in the district will open the ballot box and require that the entire vote be counted by persons designated by the judge or court. The petition must be accompanied by a deposit of fifty dollars which is returned if fraud or error is discovered. The fifty dollars is given to the county if no fraud or error is revealed. Candidates involved in a recount must be notified and can be present at the recount. Ballot boxes may be opened at any time within four months of the election. The same procedure is followed for voting machines, except that any recount must take place within twenty days of the election.

Protection Against Fraud

The Pennsylvania election code contains many laws designed to protect the election process from fraud by election officers, voters, or candidates. Illegal activities include electioneering inside the polls, bribery, candidates promising appointment to public office, unlawful possession of ballots, forging or destroying ballots, and tampering with machines.

Penalties listed in the election code include both fines and prison terms. For candidates violating the election laws, the penalty is disqualification from ever holding office in the Commonwealth. Any person who willfully violates the election laws, in addition to other penalties, is disenfranchised for ten years.

Pennsylvania's Political Parties

Active participation in a political party is one of the most effective ways for citizens to make their voices heard in government. Political parties are as much a part of modern democracy as the legislative, executive, and judicial branches of government. Organized on local, state, and national levels, the parties provide a mechanism for citizens to agree upon candidates and the programs and policies they wish the government to pursue.

Political parties in Pennsylvania operate under the rules and regulations set forth in the Registration Code and election laws of the Commonwealth.

Political parties nominate candidates for political office, adopt platforms, register voters and encourage them to vote, and, when successful at the polls, provide administrative personnel for appointment to offices in the government. Historically the United States has tended to be dominated by two political parties: the Democrats and the Republicans. Each party embraces a wide range of view-

FOUR-YEAR ELECTION CYCLE

	General Election Even-numbered year	Municipal Election Odd-numbered year	General Election Even-numbered year	Municipal Election Odd-numbered year
FEDERAL	President and Vice-President U.S. Senator (c) Representative (a) in Congress		U.S. Senator (c) Representative (a) in Congress	
STATE	Attorney General Auditor General Treasurer Senator in the General Assembly Representative (a) in the General Assembly Justices and State Judges (d,e)	Justice (d), Supreme Court Judge (d), Superior and Commonwealth Courts Judge (d), Court of Common Pleas District Justice (c)	Governor/Lt. Governor Senator in the General Assembly Representative (a) in the General Assembly Justices and State Judges (d,e)	Justice (d), Supreme Court Judge (d), Superior and Commonwealth Courts Judge (d), Court of Common Pleas District Justice (c)
COUNTY		Sheriff Coroner Jury Commissioner		Commissioners District Attorney Register of Wills Controller Treasurer Clerk of Courts Prothonotary Recorder of Deeds

MUNICIPAL (f)	Mayor	
	Council, cities and boroughs	Council, cities and boroughs
	Commissioners, first-class township	Commissioners, first-class township
	Supervisors (c), second-class township	Supervisors (c) second-class township
	Treasurer	Controller, second-class city
	Tax collector	Treasurer, third-class city
	Auditor (c)	Auditor (c)
	Controller, third-class cities, some boroughs and townships	School Directors (b)
	School Directors (b)	Constables (c,g)
	Constable	
ELECTION DISTRICT	Judge of Election	
	Majority Inspector	
	Minority Inspector	
ELECTED IN PRIMARY	Committee member (a), one man, one woman, from each party	Committee member (a), one man, one woman, from each party
	Delegates and Alternates to National Party Conventions	State Party Committee (a)
	State Party Committee	

KEY: The term is four years unless otherwise specified.

a. two-year term
b. four-year term, not all elected at same time
c. six-year term
d. ten-year term
e. Although justices and judges are usually elected at municipal elections (odd-numbered years), statewide judges may be elected in even-numbered years if a vacancy occurs.
f. For Home Rule municipalities, consult Home Rule Charter for information on officials to be elected and their terms of office.
g. Constables are officers of the court, not municipal officers, but are elected from municipal districts.

points yet at election time the various components of each party usually work together for the purpose of electing their candidates.

Organization of Political Parties in Pennsylvania

The most direct citizen link with a political party is through the election district and the two persons elected to serve on the district committee.

District Committee

At the primary in even-numbered years each party in every district elects one man and one woman as members of the district committee. They serve as political party representatives, to contact and represent party members within their jurisdiction. In some areas the next step in party organization is the ward. All members of the election-district committee are members of the ward and the city, township, or borough committee.

County Committee

Each party has a county committee made up of all members of district committees within the county. The county chair, whose position can be very powerful, is usually elected at a formal meeting of the committee, except for situations in which the chair is elected by the voters at the primary. The county committee may make rules for the governance of the party within the county so long as they are consistent with state law and the rules of the state party. A certified copy of the rules must be filed with the county board of elections before the rules can become effective.

State Committee

Pennsylvania law requires that every political party have a state committee vested with the general supervision, regulation, and direction of the party throughout the state. Members of state committee are elected at the primary in even-numbered years as prescribed by the rules of each party. The state committee is required to organize itself no later than the sixth Wednesday following its selection. It elects its own officers including a state chairman and vice-chairman. Its rules for governing the party must be consistent with state law. Before the state party rules can become effective, a certified copy must be filed in the office of the Secretary of the Commonwealth.

National Committee

The highest level of party organization is the national committee, whose members are nominated by the state committee and elected by the national convention. The national committee conducts the national convention and the presidential campaign and raises money to finance party activities.

Minor Political Parties

Pennsylvania election law includes provisions for recognition of minor political organizations.

A minor political party is a qualified political

party without sufficient numbers of registered electors to enable its candidates to circulate nomination petitions. Consequently, minor political parties do not conduct primaries but circulate and file nomination papers in order to nominate candidates directly to the November ballot. Some minor parties have existed for a number of years and continue to reappear on the ballot in Pennsylvania though their overall percentage of the vote remains small. The largest minor party in recent years has been the Consumer party.

A political body is a political organization that is unable to meet political party qualifications. Political body candidates are often referred to as "independents" because they are not sponsored by a bona fide political party. They too must circulate and file nomination papers to get on the ballot. Independents who run on their own are usually visible for only one election.

A few minor political parties have had an effect on the system in that positions they espoused were sometimes later incorporated into the platforms of other parties. When that happened, the minor party usually ceased to exist.

Nominations for Office

Nominations for political office are made either by nomination petition or by nomination papers.

Nomination Petition

Political party candidates are nominated at primaries. With a nomination petition, it is relatively simple to get a candidate's name on the party's ballot in the primary, with or without party backing. Signatures required on petitions range from five to one thousand depending on the office concerned and the population of the governmental unit. Petitions may be circulated not earlier than the thirteenth Tuesday prior to the primary, nor later than the tenth Tuesday. The petitions must be filed on or before the tenth Tuesday preceding the primary.

Citizens wishing to run for public office must pay a fee (except candidates for school board and any other office that pays no salary) and file, along with the petition, an affidavit stating their residence, election district, and the name of the office for which they are a candidate. They must also state that they are eligible for the office and that they will not knowingly violate any provisions of laws regulating nominations and election expenses. Candidates for Common Pleas Court, district justice, or school board director may cross-file, which means that they may file a petition under more than one political party label. Candidates for state, county, or local office must swear or affirm a loyalty oath. Candidates for federal office and political party office are no longer required to do so because of a United States Supreme Court decision.

Nomination Papers

Candidates of minor political parties and "independent" candidates are nominated by nomination papers to run in the November election. These candidates must disaffiliate from any political party and may not have been a candidate for any office in the preceding primary.

The number of signatures on the nomination papers must equal two percent of the largest vote cast for any elected state candidate in the last election. For all other offices, the number of signatures must equal two percent of the largest vote cast for any elected officer (except judge) at the last election in the district in which the candidate is running. The number, however, is not to be less than the number required for nomination petitions for party candidates for the same office.

If at the previous November election one of the political body's candidates polls at least two percent statewide and two percent in ten counties of the largest entire vote cast in the state for any elected candidate, then that body is entitled to nominate candidates in the next primary election. The political body may qualify at the county level when one of its candidates polls at least five percent of the largest entire vote cast for any elected candidate in that county. It would then be able to enter a slate in that county in the following primary.

Independent candidates not affiliated with any political party or body may also run on the November ballot with requirements similar to those for political bodies. They must choose a name for the nomination papers, such as "Citizens for Doe."

Candidates for government study commissions, a nonpartisan office, file papers in the same manner as other candidates but do not list a political party on their papers.

Any candidate who has run in the primary and lost may not subsequently file nomination papers in the same year unless for an office that did not appear on the primary ballot, such as a special election to fill a vacancy.

Candidates for various offices may be nominated by one nomination paper, provided that each political body does not nominate more candidates than there are offices to be voted for, and that all signers are qualified to vote for all of the candidates thus nominated. When filing nomination papers, a candidate must pay a filing fee and include an affidavit similar to that which accompanies nomination petitions. Nomination papers must be circulated and filed between the tenth Wednesday prior to the election and August 1.

Restrictions on Political Activity

The federal Hatch Act and state civil service laws limit the partisan political activities of certain government employees under civil service. They may not be active in any political party, may not circulate petitions, may not be at the polling place on election day except to vote, and may not hold elective office.

The only other restrictions on political activity in the Commonwealth refer to incompatible offices; for instance, teachers may not serve on the school board in the district in which they are employed.

According to the State Ethics Act, "the people of this state have a right to be assured that the financial interests of holders of or candidates for public office do not conflict with the public trust." The act requires financial disclosure by all candidates for state, county, and local public office before filing nomination petitions or papers. Candidates must also submit campaign expense reports periodically to the state or county election bureau, depending on the office sought. A statement of financial interest must also be filed by certain appointed public officials except candidates for advisory boards or commissions. The individual must list sources of income over $500 (but not the amount), creditors, gifts, business directorships, or other financial interests.

Financial Disclosure

Campaign Finance Law

Each candidate is given the complete text of the Political Campaign Expense Account Reporting Law at the time a petition is filed. This law is extensive and complicated and does not lend itself to easy summary. Pennsylvania sets no limit on campaign expenditures or individual contributions to local, statewide, or party committees. The Commonwealth mandates the accounting of receipts and expenditures. Periodic reporting is required. (Candidates running for federal offices are restricted, according to federal law, on the raising of funds and a maximum is placed on contributions and expenditures.)

While political contributions to a candidate or party by corporations, unincorporated associations, and labor unions are prohibited, these organizations can form political action committees (PACs) through which employees, stockholders, members, and the families of all of these may contribute. Political action committees must operate under the same reporting rules as other political committees.

Legitimate expenses for campaigns include maintenance and furnishing of offices, employment of office help, printing, travel, postage, advertising, rent, employment of poll watchers, transportation of voters, and legal counsel.

Within thirty days following the primary or general election, a candidate or treasurer of a political committee must file an accounting of all money received, contributed, or disbursed, the date of transaction, and the name of the person from whom monies are received or to whom paid. In addition, the candidate or committee treasurer must declare the purpose for which money was disbursed.

When the total, certifiable receipts or disbursements and liabilities of a candidate or political committee do not exceed $250, no accounting is necessary. Candidates with no contributions, disbursements, or liabilities do not need to file a statement if they execute the Waiver of Expense Account Reporting affidavit when they file their nominating petitions.

It is illegal for any candidate to disburse money received from an anonymous source. Such funds must be turned over to the State Treasurer. Periodic expense reports must be filed with the Secretary of the Commonwealth for statewide elections and with the county board of elections for local elections.

Elected candidates may not take office until their accounts have been filed. The law requires records to be held for three years. All accounts are open to public inspection in the office where they are filed. The penalties for noncompliance with the campaign reporting law are severe, involving both fines and imprisonment. Candidates found in violation of this law are disqualified from holding office in the Commonwealth.

For further information on topics in this chapter, see the following sources in *Key to Further Information:*

All About Elections in Pennsylvania

League of Women Voters of Pennsylvania

8

Economic Development

Economic change in Pennsylvania has mirrored national trends during the last decade. In the 1970s the state led the nation in the production of pig iron and steel and manufacturing accounted for 90 percent of the value of goods produced in the state. Lack of capital investment in heavy industry, outmoded and inefficient production capacity, and chronically high unemployment depressed the state's economy during the 1970s and early 1980s. Despite the effects of the dramatic downturn in heavy industry, the state's economy began to recover in the second half of the 1980s. Four key factors facilitated economic redirection:

- accessible domestic markets with 52 percent of the United States population within 500 miles
- inexpensive and abundant energy resources with the largest production of natural gas in the Northeast, and the third largest coal and electricity output in the United States
- one of the most extensive transportation net-

works in the nation, including the major inland ports of Erie, Pittsburgh, and Philadelphia
■ an available work force

Pennsylvania has a stable tax rate and ranks twenty-second in per capita taxation based on both state and local revenues as a percent of total income. This is well below the national average.

Agriculture is the state's largest industry, annually generating $35 billion in economic activity. Sales of crops and livestock contribute $3 billion of that total. Pennsylvania has the largest rural population in the United States.

In 1986 jobs in the service sector accounted for 25 percent of employment, wholesale and retail trade 23 percent, and manufacturing 22 percent.

The state's per capita expenditure on economic development is among the nation's highest and is directed through the departments of Commerce, Transportation, Agriculture, Community Affairs, Labor and Industry, and Education.

Economic Development Partnership/ Department of Commerce

In 1987, the governor, through executive order, created the Economic Development Partnership. This organization, which is an integral part of the Department of Commerce, has a mission to create and maintain jobs in Pennsylvania, improve the productivity of new and existing businesses, diversify the state's economy, and oversee public-private economic development activities. The forty-five members of the partnership provide guidance on programs operated by the Department of Commerce.

Administration

The Secretary of Commerce serves also as the Executive Director of the Economic Development Partnership and exercises authority over all phases of Department of Commerce activities. The secretary is ex-officio chair of Department of Commerce administered authorities, boards and commissions, and the Nursing Home Loan Agency.

Directed by a deputy secretary, the department's administration, planning, research, and program functions include economic policy analysis, administration of regional and community initiatives, and direction of the loan and bond programs.

A Deputy Secretary for Development directs and controls development efforts, including the Governor's Response Team and the offices of Technology Development, Enterprise Development, Business Assistance, and Development Packaging. The Governor's Response Team, created to assist Partnership activities, responds to priority projects involving plant shutdowns, move-outs, expansion, and recruitment.

The Bureau of Domestic Commerce recruits new industry and assists existing Pennsylvania firms to expand their efforts. It provides information about the domestic economic development programs of the Commonwealth.

The Business Resource Network is a clearinghouse to help small businesses find resources and services. It provides advocacy for small businesses, helps formulate positions on key small-business issues, and monitors the impact of proposed legislation.

Export trade and foreign investment in Pennsylvania business and industry is fostered by the Bureau of International Development.

Budget

Primary funding for economic development activities comes from the general fund and comprises 1.5 percent of the total state budget. Less than 3 percent of the Commerce budget comes from federal or other sources. The budget has increased 400 percent in the 1980s, from $28.7 million in 1979–80 to $515 million in 1987–88.

The legislature appropriates money from the general fund to offset revenue losses in the event of a recession (Rainy Day Fund) and to alleviate unemployment by attracting large industrial manufacturing or research-and-development plants (Sunny Day Fund.)

Business Loan and Grant Programs

The state has many financial assistance programs designed to encourage economic development and promote job creation. Most are fashioned to meet very specific needs.

During the last thirty years, the Pennsylvania Industrial Development Authority (PIDA) has stimulated business activity in areas of high unemployment through long-term, low-interest loans to firms engaged in manufacturing or industrial enterprises. PIDA funds may be used for land and for building construction or renovation. Special incentives are given to small businesses and advanced-technology firms and companies located in state-designated enterprise zones. A qualified business may receive a loan up to $1.5 million, with interest rates ranging from 3.0 percent to 7.5 percent, depending upon the unemployment rate in the county where the project is located.

Financing for projects approved through the

Revenue Bond and Mortgage Program (RBMP) is secured from private-sector sources. These funds are borrowed through a local industrial development authority. Because the authority is recognized as a political subdivision, the lender does not pay taxes on interest earned from the loan (except for those projects eliminated by the 1986 Federal Tax Act) and the borrower has the benefit of an interest rate lower than conventional rates. Eligible projects must be approved by the federal as well as the state government. Businesses can use the funds to acquire land, buildings, machinery, and new equipment.

A corporation that is not making a profit may receive a 20 percent tax credit for the purchase of new or used equipment or for plant expansion within the state under special conditions.

The Ben Franklin Partnership program funds research and development projects designed to benefit Pennsylvania's economy through the development and commercialization of advanced technologies. Four advanced-technology centers operate as consortia for private sector, labor, economic development groups, and institutions of higher education. As part of the Ben Franklin Partnership program, the Seed Venture Capital Fund provides capital for start-up firms. Preference is given to firms with fifty or fewer employees, and the grant, up to $35,000, must be matched by a three-to-one private investment.

The Pennsylvania Capital Loan Fund (PCLF) provides low-interest loans to businesses for capital-development projects that result in long-term net new employment opportunities. The PCLF is capitalized with federal funds from the Appalachian Regional Commission, the Economic Development Administration, and state appropriations. In 1987 the program was expanded to provide assistance to apparel manufacturers and to small-business enterprises that penetrate or increase their penetration of foreign export markets. Eligibility criteria, terms, and rates differ depending on the funding source.

The Small Business Incubator Loan Program funds the development of incubator facilities that provide new manufacturing or product-development companies with the space and business-development services needed to start up and survive in the early years of business growth.

Small Business Development Centers provide assistance and advice for starting small businesses and obtaining licenses and funding.

Specific infrastructure improvements necessary to complement industrial investment by private companies are funded through the Business Infrastructure Development (BID) program. Qualifying improvements to facilities include construction related to energy conservation, fire and safety, sewer and water, and transportation and waste disposal. Grants and loans are awarded to local sponsors. Private companies eligible for assistance by local sponsors include agricultural, industrial, manufacturing and research, and development enterprises.

The Pennsylvania Minority Business Development Authority (PMBDA) enhances business opportunities for minorities by providing technical, managerial, and financial assistance to eligible individuals and businesses. PMBDA offers low-interest, long-term loans and equity investment guarantees in the start-up or expansion of minority-owned businesses. In 1985, PMBDA established the Surety Bond Guarantee and Working Capital Loan programs to guarantee up to 90 percent of bid and performance bonds needed by a minority business to obtain a contract with a state agency, and to provide short-term loans for working capital to minority contractors with the state.

The Nursing Home Loan Agency (NHLA) provides financing for the state's nursing homes and personal-care boarding homes, enabling them to comply with the life-safety code standards and/or fire and panic code standards. The agency offers low-interest loans to eligible nursing homes and personal care boarding homes unable to obtain financing from conventional sources. The law also permits financing for the conversion of unneeded hospital beds into nursing home beds. The interest rate varies according to the bond market and federal tax regulations.

Employee Ownership Assistance Program (EOAP) provides funds for feasibility studies and technical assistance to employee groups considering the ownership of a firm. The governor may transfer funds into the operating assistance segment of the program from any other economic development program on an as-needed basis.

Community Programs

Economically distressed municipalities, especially those communities that have experienced major plant closings, can be granted funds to develop local economic-recovery strategies and marketing plans from the Pennsylvania Economic Revitalization Fund (PERF).

Pennsylvania Economic Development Financing Authority (PEDFA) offers pooled bond issues for both tax-exempt and taxable bonds as loans to local industrial and commercial development authorities for economic development projects.

Local municipalities can receive grants through the Site Development program to repair or construct water and sewer facilities (excluding sewage treatment) and access-road projects. Municipalities with a population of fewer than 12,000 are eligible for similar loans through the Community Facilities program.

The state encourages regional solutions to economic problems through special regional organizations. In the Beaver, Lower Monongahela, Mid-Monongahela, and Shenango River valleys, the Steel Valley Assistance program provides the framework for an independent decision-making consortia.

Transportation

A healthy economy demands a strong transportation network. The Department of Transportation has the responsibility to develop programs to assure adequate, safe and efficient transportation facilities and services at the lowest reasonable cost to the citizenry. It plans, designs, constructs, and maintains Pennsylvania's multimodal transportation system. It assists local and regional transit systems through funding for operations and capital assistance. The state system has more than 43,000 miles of roads and highways, 25,000 bridges, and three state-owned airports. Principal sources of revenue are liquid-fuel taxes, motor license fees, and federal aid.

The department is organized into central office engineering bureaus and twelve statewide engineering districts. Each district is responsible for carrying out department policies.

Agriculture

The agricultural industry employs nearly 1.2 million persons, about one-fifth of the state's work force. Milk, apples, sheep, tobacco, grains, mushrooms, ice cream, chickens, flowering plants, and many other foods, animals, and plants are part of Pennsylvania's diverse agricultural industry. These products are raised or grown on 8.7 million acres of farm land. The industry, cushioned by this diversity and proximity to markets, has not been as hard hit as the rest of the nation by falling farm prices and rising costs. It is difficult, however, for many farmers to make a fair living at farming. About 80 percent of farm families have at least one member working in a nonfarm job in order maintain their standard of living.

The Department of Agriculture administers financial programs to provide economic incentive to the industry. The Agricultural Entrepreneur Development Program helps finance new or expanded agricultural processing facilities. To be eligible a project must use or add value to farm commodities grown in the state. The Farm Market Loan program makes low-interest loans to family farmers to finance facilities for marketing their products.

Other Economic Development Programs

The Enterprise Zone program, federally funded and implemented through the Department of Community Affairs (DCA), provides special funding for business development in low income communities. In Pennsylvania these programs are administered through independent nonprofit corporations. The program provides low-interest loans to start-up and expanding businesses.

Through the Neighborhood Assistance program, the first of its kind in the country, the Department of Community Affairs grants tax credits to corporations who assist nonprofit organizations to develop comprehensive programs that assist a community with economic revitalization. Contributions may be cash, technical assistance, or equipment.

The Department of General Services Office of Minority and Women Business Enterprise, established in 1987, increases minority business activity by assisting minorities and women to obtain state contracts.

The Department of Education administers a number of adult basic education and training programs designed to enhance workers' skills. (See chapter 9, Education.) It administers the state-funded Customized Job Training program, which makes funds available to businesses to offset the cost of training new employees at the work site.

The federally funded Job Training Partnership Act (JTPA) is administered in Pennsylvania through twenty-seven regional Private Industry Councils. JTPA provides job training and cash incentives aimed at matching skilled employees with the employers' needs.

Citizen Participation

The Pennsylvania Economic Development Partnership is a statewide coalition of forty-five members who are leaders in Pennsylvania business, labor, education, and government. The partnership develops strategies to use Pennsylvania's resources to achieve economic growth.

A Transportation Commission and a Transportation Advisory Committee, made up of representatives from industry, citizen interest groups, and the legislature, evaluate programs, study highway and mass-transit issues, and assist the department in setting transportation priorities.

For further information on topics in this chapter, see the following sources in *Key to Further Information:*

Pennsylvania Chamber of Business and Industry

Pennsylvania Economy League

9

Education

Pennsylvania has the eighth largest public school system in the nation and leads in the number of post-secondary vocational/technical schools. These institutions serve 2.6 million students.

Responsibility for providing a system of public education has been vested in the Pennsylvania legislature since the first state constitution was drafted in 1776. It was not until the passage of the Free School Act in 1834, however, that the public education system began to develop. According to the present constitution, the legislature continues to bear primary responsibility for educating the citizens of Pennsylvania. Article III, Section 14 states:

> The general assembly shall provide for the maintenance and support of a thorough and efficient system of public education to serve the needs of the Commonwealth.

The General Assembly is further directed by the constitution to classify school districts according to population and to set debt limits of all school districts, except Philadelphia.

The Pennsylvania Constitution establishes the office of Secretary of Education (called the Superintendent of Public Instruction until 1969) as part of the Executive Department of the Commonwealth. The governor is required to appoint a Secretary of Education, subject to consent of the Senate. Laws relating to public education are found in the Pennsylvania Public School Code of 1949.

State Board of Education

The concept of a citizen board to manage public education goes back to the late 1800s. The first State Board of Education (SBE) was created in 1911 and statutory authority followed in the Pennsylvania Administrative Code of 1929.

The SBE has the specific duty to provide direction for educational programs. It is authorized to conduct research on educational issues, hold hearings, and establish regulations, standards, policies, and guidelines for all public and private schools in Pennsylvania.

Twenty-one citizens serve on the State Board of Education. Seventeen are appointed by the governor and confirmed by the state senate. The remaining four members are the majority and minority chairs of the House and Senate education committees.

For operational purposes, ten members are assigned to the Council of Basic Education and ten to the Council of Higher Education. The Secretary of Education is the chief executive officer of the board but has no vote. The chairperson of the board and the chairperson of the two councils are gubernatorial appointees. The SBE meets six times a year and submits an annual report of activities to the governor and the General Assembly.

The Council of Basic Education establishes policy in all aspects of elementary and secondary education and is mandated to develop a master plan for basic education. The Council of Higher Education sets standards for granting post secondary certificates and degrees, develops policy proposals for community colleges and technical institutes, and is responsible for the master plan for higher education in Pennsylvania. State board members also serve as the State Board of Vocational Education, which sets policy for the development of vocational and technical education.

Members receive no salary but are entitled to reimbursement for travel and other necessary expenses in connection with their duties as board members. All terms are for six years.

Pennsylvania Department of Education

The Department of Education (PDE) is an administrative agency of the executive branch. The PDE carries out the policies of the state board and is responsible for administering the school laws of Pennsylvania. It provides leadership and services to elementary, secondary, and higher educational institutions in the state. Specific responsibilities include the following:

- Administering the school laws of Pennsylvania
- Administering rules and regulations of the State Board of Education
- Assisting local school districts in their educational programs
- Evaluating programs of instruction and prescribing minimum courses of study

- Apportioning state appropriations for education to local school districts
- Contracting with and distributing funds to nonpublic schools for the purchase of secular educational services
- Promoting and assisting in the establishment of community colleges and providing services to other institutions of higher education
- Conducting educational research projects
- Licensing and regulating private schools
- Approving programs of proprietary post-secondary institutions (licensed business and technical schools)
- Administering and supervising cooperative programs with private and other state and federal agencies
- Collecting and publishing information about education in the Commonwealth
- Administering the state program for public libraries

The Secretary of Education, as chief administrative officer, is assisted by a deputy secretary in executive and administrative matters and an executive assistant. A commissioner for basic education, also appointed by the governor, is responsible for elementary and secondary programs and support services and for special and vocational education. A commissioner for higher education directs the evaluation of higher-education programs and teacher preparation and certification. These two commissioners provide information and reports to their respective state board councils.

School Districts

The school district is governed by the school board, which, because it is considered a unit of local government, has the power to tax and incur debt. Historically, school-district and municipal boundaries were often identical. In the early 1960s the General Assembly began to look at ways to reduce local district cost and increase efficiency. One approach was school consolidation. Under Act 299 of 1963 amending the School Code of 1949, districts with enrollments under 5,000 students were ordered to consolidate with contiguous districts. The outcome of this act was the reduction in the number of local districts from 2,056 in 1963 to 501 in 1988.

Board of School Directors

Pennsylvania's educational system is administered locally by local boards of nine directors in accordance with Section 301 of the Public School Code. They serve as local legislative bodies for public education and act as an extension of the state legislature. They make decisions on a wide range of concerns such as curriculum, staff, school buildings, and textbooks. Local educational policies must be consistent with the laws enacted by the legislature.

In every school district (except Philadelphia), members of the school board are elected at the municipal election. The Philadelphia school board is appointed by the mayor from a list of qualified candidates prepared by a nonpartisan nominating panel. In order to be qualified as a school director, a person must be of good moral standing, at least eighteen years of age, and a resident of the school district for at least one year prior to election or appointment. School boards have the responsibility for planning, setting policy, and evaluating school operations. They adopt rules and regulations to govern their own affairs and the conduct of employees.

School board members campaign for election on a partisan basis, but they may cross-file under more than one political party label. Several directors are elected at each municipal election. When a vacancy occurs, the local board must appoint a new director within thirty days. If such appointment is not made, the public has the right to petition the Court of Common Pleas to fill the vacancy.

All school boards, except Philadelphia, have the fiscal autonomy to establish budgets and levy taxes to support these budgets. In Philadelphia, because the board is appointed, funds for education are appropriated by the elected city council as part of the city budget. The fiscal year of all boards, except Pittsburgh and Scranton, is July 1 to June 30.

School boards appoint a district superintendent as the chief administrative officer of the school district. This person must meet specified educational and employment criteria and receive a commission from the Secretary of Education. The superintendent's contract can be three, four, or five years. It is the superintendent's duty to carry out the policies of both state and local school boards and to suggest improvements in district operations.

Intermediate Units

An increased awareness of specialized educational needs such as vocational-technical educational and special programs for disadvantaged students occurred in the late 1960s. Even larger districts, created through school consolidation, could not afford sophisticated supplementary and ancillary services, nor was it practical for the state to administer them. In response the 1971 General Assembly established twenty-nine regional educational service agencies, called Intermediate Units (IU), that were empowered to provide support services to the local districts.

Consultative and direct program services are provided to public and nonpublic schools by the IU. Such services may include instructional seminars, material centers (which lend projectors, films and filmstrips, and books, along with curriculum information), educational broadcasting, health programs, transportation, data processing, vocational-technical assistance, and coordinated purchasing and research. Local districts receive help to develop liaisons with institutions of higher learning and to provide teachers for reading, speech, and special education, as well as visual and psychological services. The IU also administers the federally funded Head Start programs.

Intermediate Units are financed in large part by the state's general operating funds. Other revenue comes from local school districts, which share the costs of the IU and pay for services provided by the IU on their behalf. These Intermediate Units are governed by boards drawn from the elected school boards of the constituent districts.

Financing Education

Pennsylvania's public school expenditures in 1987–88 totaled over $3.8 billion and represented about 37 percent of the state budget. The federal government provides funding for special programs for educationally deprived children and adults. Chapter I of the Education Consolidation and Improvement Act (ECIA) is the largest of these programs and provides funds for supplementary and remedial programs in math and reading.

Local School Financing

School districts are given the taxing authority to support their schools. In 1987–88, 77.1 percent of local tax revenue for schools was raised from real estate taxes, .05 percent from per capita taxes, and 13.5 percent from Act 511 taxes (the Local Tax Enabling Act of 1965). Remaining local revenue was derived from delinquent taxes, payments in lieu of taxes, and special taxes in Philadelphia and Pittsburgh. (See chapter 5, Financing Government.)

State Subsidies

Pennsylvania schools are funded by a complicated state and local financial partnership established by the General Assembly. School districts receive subsidies based on pupil population and the wealth of the school district. The Equalized Subsidy for Basic Education (ESBE) provides the largest single source of funding. The subsidy formula is based on a fixed dollar amount per student, adjusted by measuring local wealth against a statewide average. Wealth is calculated by adding 60 percent of the market value of real property and 40 percent of personal income. Special problems such as high- or low-density populations or many children in low-income families are also factored into the formula.

Additional subsidies are provided for vocational education, transportation of pupils, special education, debt services, and rental payments for school construction.

During the 1986–87 school year 1,656,000 children attended public school and 112,000 attended nonpublic school. Over 3,000 school buildings were operated by public school districts and 900 by private and parochial institutions. All public school districts must provide at least 180 days of instruction per year.

Elementary and Secondary Education

Teacher Certification

The Professional Standards and Practices Commission, a sixteen-member board appointed by the governor, develops certification requirements for teachers and accreditation standards for schools of education. All professional employees teaching in public school systems must meet these standards.

In 1985 teacher-certification testing was added to the requirements governing teacher-preparation programs in Pennsylvania. Candidates who seek certification are tested to assure competence in basic skills, general and professional knowledge, and specific subject areas.

The Continuing Professional Development Act of 1986 (Act 178) requires that school districts establish two-year professional-development programs for persons not wishing to pursue professionally related master's degrees. Employees who received their teaching certificates after May 31, 1987, must participate in such programs at least once every five years. The development program does not apply to those certified prior to that date. The state can withhold funds from school districts who fail to implement professional development plans.

Collective Bargaining

The Pennsylvania Public Employee Law (Act 195, 1970) establishes the teacher's right to organize, bargain collectively, and strike. It provides for fact-finding, compulsory mediation, and a process for arbitration in case of impasses. It also defines the scope of collective bargaining.

Pennsylvania is one of seven states that allow teachers to strike. Although the number of strikes decreased during the 1980s, the duration of individual strikes increased. Statistics for the 1987–88 school year show that in the seventeen-year period since Act 195 was passed, Pennsylvania has experienced 704 school strikes. In 1984 a comprehensive study was made of the law and modifications were recommended. However, a five-member Senate Task Force could not reach agreement on the changes and in 1988 the act remains as written.

Curriculum

Public school curriculum is affected by state law, by State Board of Education regulations, by Department of Education guidelines, and by local school board decisions. Local boards have the power to arrange specific courses that conform to state laws and regulations and that supplement minimum state requirements.

Courses in elementary schools include English, spelling, reading and writing, arithmetic, geography, history of the United States and Pennsylvania, loyalty to the state and national governments, safety education, humane treatment of birds and animals, physical education, physiology, AIDS instruction, music, art, and environmental education.

The high school curriculum was revised in 1987

to provide a stronger emphasis on mathematics, science, and English. Districts are required to offer courses in computer science. Graduation requirements were strengthened from thirteen credits in three years to twenty-one in four years.

Kindergarten

Pennsylvania law states that schools must be provided for children from the ages of six years to twenty-one or graduation, whichever comes first. School boards are permitted, but not required, to set up and maintain kindergartens for children between the ages of four and six. Once established, kindergartens become an integral part of the elementary school system and must remain open for at least two and one-half hours a day for the full school term. Every public school district has a kindergarten program.

Public School Libraries

Each district is required to have a library book collection of no fewer than 10 titles per elementary and secondary pupil, or a collection of 10,000 titles, whichever is less. Books borrowed from non-school libraries may not be counted. School districts must employ a full-time certified elementary teacher or certified school librarian to develop an effective library system for the elementary schools in the district. Every secondary school is required to employ a full-time certified school librarian.

Student Evaluation

Act 299 of 1963 assigned the State Board of Education the responsibility "to develop . . . an evaluation procedure designed to measure objectively the adequacy and efficiency of the educational programs offered by the public schools of the Commonwealth." The educational quality assessment (EQA) program evolved from this charge. The method of evaluation includes tests to measure the achievement and performance of students in all subjects and courses. Twelve goals of quality education, developed by the State Board of Education, form the basis for the EQA program. Using EQA and the data provided, each school district can compare its effectiveness with other schools in the state that operate under similar circumstances. This assessment is not mandatory for school districts and individual students can decline to participate.

The Tests for Essential Learning Skills (TELS) are administered yearly to third-, fifth-, and eighth-grade students. All districts are required to develop special remedial curricula for students who score below the statewide mean.

Special Education

The purpose of special education in Pennsylvania is to provide a free and appropriate public education for exceptional children to prepare them for productive lives as full citizens.

Pennsylvania law defines exceptional children as those persons who deviate from the average in physical, mental, emotional, or social characteristics to such an extent that they require special facilities or services. They may be visually and/or hearing impaired, physically handicapped, learning disabled, mentally retarded, brain damaged, speech and language impaired, socially and emotionally disturbed, or mentally gifted and talented. All children in detention homes are also classified as exceptional. The Bureau of Special Education administers a statewide program of special educational services for exceptional persons.

Local school districts are responsible for the education of all exceptional children living in their districts. If the local district cannot provide appropriate services, the intermediate unit is the provider. In some cases the state may provide classes in a local building for children with the most severe handicaps. Ninety-five percent of the exceptional children are served in public school buildings. During the 1987 school year more than 265,000 exceptional children were enrolled in special classes throughout the Commonwealth.

In Pennsylvania, placements in special education classes are determined annually by a multidisciplinary educational team. An individualized education program (IEP) must be developed for each student. Parents must be notified of the placement, have the right to review all documents related to the placement, and may appeal the placement decision if they believe it is inappropriate.

The state offers a continuum of services through a variety of providers. Special education resource teachers provide support materials for regular classroom teachers. Social workers and psychologists offer consultation and counseling. Four types of organizational patterns are available: full-time special education classes; part-time classes; resource rooms; and itinerant services provided by a specialist who comes as needed.

Federal legislation in 1975 (Act 94–142) had a significant impact on the way services are delivered to handicapped students. This law mandated that free and appropriate public education services be offered as close to the student's home as possible, in the least restrictive environment appropriate for the disability, and that parents have the right to due process in the determination of their child's placement. Further, handicapped children should be educated with children who are not handicapped unless an overwhelming objection is raised against it.

Mentally gifted students are defined by the Department of Education as having "outstanding intellectual and creative ability, the development of which requires special activities or services not ordinarily provided in the regular program." The standards for mentally gifted state: "Persons shall be assigned to a program for the gifted when they have an IQ score of 130 or higher. A limited number of persons with IQ scores lower than 130 may be admitted to gifted programs when other educational criteria in the person's profile strongly indicate gifted ability."

The State of Pennsylvania sponsors five-week summer school programs in the arts, sciences, international studies, agriculture, and business for gifted and talented high school students.

Early Intervention

Action to provide early-intervention programs for preschool age children was initiated by the state in 1986. This program provides early detection of children at risk of academic difficulty because of physical or mental handicaps or negative home circumstances, and develops appropriate intervention plans for these children. All intermediate units operate early-intervention programs for handicapped children.

The departments of Education, Health, and Welfare combine resources to track children who are identified as handicapped or who are in the population considered at risk. Public and private providers offer services to both parents and children.

Children of Migrant Workers

Children of migrant workers are subject to compulsory school regulations and must attend school in the district in which they are currently residing. Fifty-three counties receive subsidies for migrant education programs. The federally funded Pennsylvania Migrant Education Program (PMEP), which is the thirteenth largest in the country, is administered by the Department of Education and operated locally. Seven local agencies, including three state universities, three Intermediate Units, and one school district, provide a variety of support services. Preventive health care, psychological counseling, and career education are available to migrant children. Local school districts receive $100 per day for up to forty days for each migratory child. This is usually a summer program.

Pennsylvania participates in the Migrant Student Record Transfer System, a computerized communications network designed to transfer educational and medical records of migrant students as they move from school to school.

PMEP has received six national project grants that range from funding to develop a resource database to a contract to identify appropriate teacher recruitment techniques as well as to implement a pilot training program for teacher recruiters. Income from the sale of project services supports administrative costs for PMEP. In 1988 PMEP produced a videotape series with "Mister Rogers' Neighborhood" entitled "You Are Special," which is marketed nationwide.

Vocational and Adult Education

The State Board of Education, sitting as the State Board for Vocational Education, guides the development of vocational and technical education in Pennsylvania. The Bureau of Vocational Education makes available to persons of all ages vocational training, retraining, and continuing education courses that meet the needs of the community. The program offers training for semiskilled, skilled, and technical jobs. Particular emphasis is placed on training for the work force of the future.

Secondary school students can participate in vocational programs in their local school district or, in some cases, in area vocational-technical schools. Participating districts or intermediate units operate these schools. Eighty-five area vocational-technical schools operate in the state. Community colleges also conduct vocational-technical courses. Federal funds are available through Chapter 11 of the Educational Consolidation and Improvement Act (ECIA).

In 1986 Pennsylvania had the fourth largest number of adults in the nation who had not completed a high school education. Less than one percent of these 2,700,000 adults participated in adult basic education programs. To increase educational opportunities for this population, the General Assembly passed the Adult Literacy Act. This act establishes a grant program to fund the following services: adult education programs, training for volunteer instructors, administration, support services, and outreach services. Adult and continuing education programs include evening high school programs, manpower training, and the retraining of the unemployed and underemployed. In addition to state funds, monies are provided through the Federal Job Training and Partnership Act and the Perkins Act for vocational education.

Equal Oppportunity

Equal opportunity in education is mandated by the federal government through Title IX of the Education Amendments of 1972, the Pennsylvania Equal Rights Amendment of 1972, and State Board of Education regulations. Department of Education regulations state that discrimination because of sex is forbidden and all classes, programs, and extracurricular activities in the schools must be available to all students.

The Pennsylvania Human Relations Commission (PHRC) ensures that school segregation does not exist. The commission has established racial-balance guidelines for local school districts. The PHRC may obtain a court order to change the racial composition of schools in a given district if the complaint of segregation is substantiated and the local school board refuses to desegregate voluntarily. The Department of Education is empowered to withhold funds from any school district that fails to comply with a court order to desegregate. As a result of Human Relations Commission efforts, twenty-eight school districts have been involved in desegregation. The PHRC continues to work with school districts that fall out of compliance.

Higher Education

Higher education in Pennsylvania includes public colleges and universities owned by the state, state-related universities, state-aided institutions, community colleges, private state-aided institutions, private colleges, universities and seminaries, junior colleges, and proprietary schools. In 1987–88 more than 564,000 students were enrolled in 230 institutions of higher education authorized to grant degrees. Pennsylvania has the third largest number of higher educational institutions in the nation.

State System of Higher Education

In 1983 a system of fourteen state institutions was created to provide quality education at the lowest cost. This State System of Higher Education (SSHE) offers a broad range of undergraduate and graduate degree programs, as well as certification and continuing education studies. Eighty-nine thousand students attend system universities.

A chancellor is the chief executive officer and policy is directed by a sixteen-member board of governors appointed by the governor. Each university has its own board of trustees. Appropriations for operations are ordinary expenses of government, requiring only a majority vote of each house.

State-Related Universities

Through separate legislative acts, the state has established special relationships with four universities: Lincoln University and Temple University located in Philadelphia, the University of Pittsburgh, and The Pennsylvania State University in State College. These schools receive special, non-preferred appropriations that must be approved by a two-thirds vote for approval.

The Pennsylvania State University has been a state-related institution for over one hundred years. Established on land granted to the state by the federal government in 1862, the university is required by the Land Grant Act to provide for research, agriculture programs, and extension services. Temple University and the University of Pittsburgh became state-related in 1965 and 1966, respectively, and Lincoln University in 1973.

State-Aided Institutions

The state provides partial funding for the operation of eleven private institutions and three trade schools. These specialized schools offer post-secondary trade education and higher education in such disciplines as medicine, the arts, science, and agriculture.

Community Colleges

Community colleges, created in the Community College Act of 1963, confer associate degrees in various professional, semiprofessional, and technical occupations. They offer two years of college to a student who then can transfer to a four-year college. They also provide numerous continuing education courses in academic and nonacademic subjects. These courses enable students to gain employment in advanced technology fields through a two-year program.

The colleges, locally sponsored and administered, in most cases are financed one-third by appropriation from the county they serve, one-third state appropriation, and one-third student tuition. Fourteen counties have established community colleges.

Private Colleges, Universities, Seminaries, and Junior Colleges

Most private higher educational institutions receive some type of indirect state assistance, including student scholarship aid. These institutions include 208 private colleges, universities, junior colleges, and special-degree-granting institutions.

Proprietary Schools

Since 1971 the state has included in its higher education planning a number of licensed business and technical schools. Financed through tuition, these proprietary schools are authorized by the Secretary of Education (after program approval) to award associate degrees in specialized business or technology programs. Students are required to have a high school diploma or its equivalent for entrance and must take a minimum of sixty credits. Schools receive indirect state assistance through tax exemptions, and students are eligible for scholarship aid.

Scholarship Aid

In conformity with Pennsylvania law that there should be no financial barriers to higher education, the 1964 General Assembly created the Pennsylvania Higher Education Assistance Agency (PHEAA). PHEAA is a private corporation independent of the state executive governed by a twenty-member board. It is responsible for the administration of the federal Guaranteed Student Loan Program and the State Grant Program. During the 1986–87 school year the agency processed more than 240,000 loans equaling over $500 million in educational assistance and provided 110,000 students with grants averaging $1,000. Eligibility to participate in either program is based on financial need.

PHEAA provides Institutional Assistance Grants to private schools not eligible for state appropriations. The institution can receive an average of $650 to $750 per student.

The Scholars in Education Award Program, the Loan Forgiveness Program, and Science Teacher

Education Program, run by PHEAA, provide financial incentives for students studying science or math. These programs are funded by PHEAA's income from sale of the computer services to other states.

Tax exempt bonds, floated by PHEAA, fund the Higher Education Loan Program (HELP) and the Health Education Assistance Loans (HEALS). Persons who meet certain educational as well as income criteria can apply for these loans. The state guarantees loan repayment to private lenders in both these programs.

State Library System

The State Library is administered from within the Department of Education. Its policies are reviewed by a twelve-member Advisory Council on Library Development appointed by the governor for four-year terms. The council approves all rules and regulations and makes recommendations on the State Library and the Commonwealth library program.

The State Library provides library services to divisions, agencies, and personnel of state government, and to any resident of the Commonwealth. The State Library coordinates statewide financial assistance for public libraries; operates a reference service and interlibrary loan system; and maintains visual aid, newspaper, periodical, and rare books sections. A state law library in Harrisburg is open to the public and provides advisory services to county law libraries.

In 1987 the State Library launched the Access Pennsylvania program in which library card holders can borrow books, films, records, and other library materials from participating libraries anywhere in the state if their home library joins the Access program.

State Aid to Local and Regional Libraries

State aid is available to any local library that maintains state-required standards and makes a minimum financial effort equal to one-half mill of the assessed property value for the municipalities on behalf of which it applies, or two dollars per capita for each person residing in those municipalities.

Additional state funding is available for county, district, and regional libraries. County libraries receive grants based on local county financial participation. District libraries, which maintain central book collections, offer supplementary services to local libraries and provide direct services to persons residing in the district. They receive state appropriations based on the number of persons residing in the area served.

The Free Library of Philadelphia, the Pennsylvania State University Library, Carnegie Library of Pittsburgh, and the State Library in Harrisburg are designated as Regional Resource Centers. They are authorized to acquire major research collections and must make them available to residents of the Commonwealth on a statewide basis. Each receives $100,000 per year in state funds to develop this resource.

Citizen Participation

Citizens can have direct influence on educational programs and policy through the local school board. Major board actions such as the budget, school construction, and school closings require the board to seek public comment. Board meetings and committee meetings are open to all interested persons, and local school boards, as well as the State Board of Education, must adhere to the Sunshine Law. (See chapter 2, The Executive.)

The State Board of Education is also central to citizen participation. The board solicits citizen input on a variety of educational issues through statewide hearings.

The Department of Education requires all school districts to form citizen committees to assist the district board and administration in preparation of a five-year plan to address the educational needs of the district.

For further information on topics in this chapter, see the following sources in *Key to Further Information:*

Pennsylvania School Boards Association

Pennsylvania Federation of Teachers

Pennsylvania State Education Association

10

Public Health

The state of Pennsylvania promotes and protects the good health of its residents through programs administered by six executive departments. The Pennsylvania Department of Health (DOH) has primary responsibility and is assisted by the departments of Public Welfare, Aging, Environmental Resources, Agriculture, and Labor and Industry through their special health-related functions.

Department of Health

The Department of Health (DOH) has the power to protect the health of the people of the Commonwealth and to enforce all state statutes pertaining to public health. DOH's mission is to act as a catalyst to assure that public health programs are initiated, that linkages and coalitions with community resources or agencies are built, and that community-based public health programs evolve so that high-quality health care is geographically and economically available to all state residents.

Pennsylvania citizens receive a variety of public

health services through programs of disease prevention, screening, detection and diagnosis, and education, health training, rehabilitation, and treatment activities.

Specific responsibilities of the DOH include prevention of disease; intervention and treatment programs for drug and alcohol abuse; and the enforcement of standards for quality care in nursing homes and hospitals through supervision, licensing, certification, and quality control. Department personnel enforce the following state laws: Abortion Control; Clinical Laboratory; Controlled Substance, Drug, Device, and Cosmetic; Disease Prevention and Control; Emergency Medical Services; Generic Drug; and Vital Statistics.

In addition to educating the public in general good health care, the Department of Health is involved in eradicating many diseases through research and special prevention programs.

Administration

The Department of Health is headed by a Secretary of Health who is appointed by the governor with the consent of the Senate. The Secretary appoints five deputy secretaries who direct bureaus and offices responsible for administration, public health, planning and quality assurance, drug and alcohol programs, and community health.

The Deputy Secretary for Administration maintains records on all births, deaths, incidence of disease, and accidents; provides information on health services; analyzes and disseminates data; and provides copies of birth and death certificates at a nominal fee.

Educational and preventive programs, maternal and child health programs, and emergency health services are coordinated by the Deputy Secretary for Public Health Programs.

The Deputy Secretary for Planning and Quality Assurance is authorized to determine statewide health needs, to engage in health planning and coordination, and to develop and implement health programs. The office administers state and federal regulatory programs to ensure compliance with minimum health and safety standards in licensed health-care facilities.

The Deputy Secretary for Drug and Alcohol Programs provides leadership, expertise, influence, and assistance to varied health service systems to protect and promote the health of Pennsylvanians through reducing the incidence of drug and alcohol abuse. In addition, the deputy is accountable for program coordination of the federal alcohol and drug abuse and mental health-services block grant.

The Deputy Secretary for Community Health directs and coordinates departmental programs through six regional service districts that provide a variety of public-health services in health centers, clinics, and county/municipal health departments.

Budget

The 1987–88 budget of $290,316,000 was divided into five program areas: health-support services, health research, preventive health, health treatment services, and prevention and treatment of drug and alcohol problems. Forty-three percent of the budget came from federal sources, with the largest share designated for preventive health care to promote sound health practices, reduce the need for remedial care, and reduce morbidity and mortality due to health defects and disease. Almost one-quarter of state health budget funds are expended for programs in drug and alcohol prevention, education, and treatment.

Community Health

Sixty-two state health centers and multiple clinic sites operate free to all persons. Centers are staffed by professional public health nurses and clerks. Part-time clinicians or nurse practitioners are available at clinic sites.

The district health centers have specialized staff to provide program consultation and directions: District Nurse Administrators, Public Health Physicians, Nutritionists, Physical Therapists, Public Health Educators, Dental Hygienists, Diabetes Coordinators, STD Representatives, T.B. Representatives, Epidemiologists, Chronic Disease Representatives, Immunization Specialists, and Environmental Health Specialists are all available at these community centers.

Approved county/municipal health departments are located in Allegheny, Bucks, Chester, and Erie counties and in the cities of Philadelphia, Allentown, Bethlehem, and York. They receive grants to operate their own programs. A maximum of $4.50 per capita matching funds and $1.50 in nonmatching funds is available to each department.

Control of Chronic and Communicable Diseases

Public health programs of the Department of Health include the prevention and early control of chronic diseases such as arthritis, cancer, diabetes, epilepsy, glaucoma, and heart disease. Consultation and treatment are provided for persons with black lung disease, cystic fibrosis, hemophilia, kidney disease, sickle cell anemia, and tuberculosis. Health centers also conduct AIDS testing, counseling, and education and provide high-blood-pressure screening.

Local public health workers investigate, collect data, and monitor disease outbreaks. Typical services include free vaccine against seven preventable diseases (measles, mumps, rubella, diphtheria, pertussis, tetanus, and poliomyelitis) in children and against tetanus in adults. Since 1982, Pennsylvania has required that all children, from kindergarten through grade twelve, be immunized against these diseases. To guarantee full protection against these diseases, DOH teams administered free immunizations to 150,000 school children during the 1982–83 school year.

Care for Children

Services for children cover both disease prevention and care for existing health problems.

The department holds child-health conferences, provides care for children born with birth defects, and offers financial support to clinics for children with physical handicaps. Diagnostic and treatment services are available statewide for children with speech and hearing problems.

Health centers provide well-baby clinics, prenatal and maternal care, counseling, and guidance to parents. Children with cardiac problems and cleft palates are referred to specialists for diagnosis and treatment. Children with other problems may be referred for further care to private or public practitioners through the state health centers.

The Department of Health participates with the

Departments of Education and Welfare in identifying children for early intervention programs. (See chapter 11, Human Services.)

Health Education

The Department of Health keeps professionals and consumers informed about health problems and issues. The department sponsors conferences, seminars, and workshops; distributes consumer health guides; and through advertising and programs on radio and television stresses the importance and advantages of good health habits. The department covers in its public-information program such areas as nutrition and diet, physical fitness, first aid in the home, immunization, and the dangers of smoking.

A toll-free health hotline is provided by the DOH for easily obtainable information. This service provides information on the prevention and treatment of communicable diseases and the location of health centers and nursing homes. Consumers can obtain appropriate publications in response to specific health questions. The department provides consultation in dental hygiene in public and state schools and hospitals and cooperates with the Department of Education in health education programs in schools.

Special Programs of the Department of Health

Maternal and child preventive health programs are administered by one of four bureaus in the Deputate of Public Health. The Special Supplemental Food Program for Women, Infants, and Children (WIC), funded by federal and state money, is designed to improve the nutrition and health status of low-income pregnant and postpartum women, as well as preschool children up to age five. The program provides vouchers for nutritious food and access to health care and nutrition education. Pennsylvania received a national WIC Award in 1987 for excellent performance in administrative cost management, caseload management, vendor monitoring, and nutrition services. The program is available in all sixty-seven counties and in 1987 served about 179,000 clients.

To enhance emergency medical-care delivery, the Department of Health began training and certifying Emergency Medical Services (EMS) personnel in 1982. By the end of 1987 almost 51,000 Emergency Medical Technicians (EMTs) were trained through a specialized, accredited eighty-one-hour course. In 1988 each ambulance run was required to have an EMT aboard, and when an ambulance is requested to provide advanced life support at least one paramedic or health professional is required to be present at the scene of an accident. The Emergency Medical Service program is partially funded by fines imposed on licensed drivers for moving vehicle violations.

Health Activities of Other Agencies

The Department of Public Welfare provides extensive care for the low-income sick with programs of medical assistance, homemaker care, and social services. The Commonwealth also operates six state general hospitals. (See chapter 11, Human Services.)

The Department of Aging administers the Pharmaceutical Assistance Contract of the Elderly (PACE) program, which enables low-income elderly persons to purchase prescription drugs at nominal cost. The PACE program includes a drug utilization review process designed to reduce the likelihood of taking incompatible prescription drugs.

The Department of Environmental Resources (DER) enforces environmental laws based on public health standards. The department monitors air pollution and water cleanliness; sewage and solid waste disposal systems; and inspects the sanitary conditions in public buildings. The Bureau of Community Environmental Control (CEC) is empowered to administer such programs as the Safe Drinking Water Act. CEC also conducts routine sampling for *Giardia* (a disease-producing organism) in public water supplies, monitors swimming pools and campgrounds, and inspects housing and sanitation facilities at seasonal farm workers' camps. DER also administers the State Rat Source Elimination Grant program, which helps communities eliminate rat habitats and develop control ordinances.

The health of workers is protected through enforcement of radiation level standards in industrial facilities and by safety inspections of coal mines. (See chapter 12, Natural Resources.)

The Department of Environmental Resources and the Department of Agriculture share responsibility for food inspection. DER inspects and licenses public eating and drinking places, convenience stores that prepare food, shellfish processors and distributors, bottled-water factories, and school food services. The Department of Agriculture inspects grocery stores, bakeries, processing plants, warehouses, and transportation facilities. It enforces the milk sanitation law and standards for fresh eggs and baby chicks. To protect the consumer from adulterated, impure, or misrepresented food, the department analyzes and samples foods and enforces truth-in-menu and food product labeling. The Pennsylvania Bakery Law, administered by the Department of Agriculture, requires bakers, including those producing pasta products, pretzels, potato chips, and snacks made from cornmeal, to obtain a license before selling their products in the Commonwealth. Packaging on licensed foods bears the imprint "Registered, Pennsylvania Department of Agriculture." This registration does not imply the department's approval of the product itself; it merely indicates that the baker's plant and employees meet certain specified standards regarding cleanliness in food handling.

The Department of Labor and Industry enforces fire and panic regulations in all Pennsylvania public buildings except in the cities of Philadelphia, Pittsburgh, and Scranton. It also administers the Community and Worker Right to Know Law, which makes information on hazardous substances in workplaces available to the public.

The Bureau of Professional and Occupational Affairs in the Department of State licenses individuals engaged in health-related professional services such as dentists and chiropractors, and personal-service providers such as beauticians and nursing home administrators. Examinations are required by the department before licenses are issued.

Citizen Participation

A twelve-member nonsalaried Advisory Board of Health is responsible for adopting rules and regulations necessary to carry out legislative mandates. The DOH also involves citizens as members of the seventeen legislatively or federally mandated advisory boards and the seven specialty boards established by the governor's executive order. Two programs developed by advisory boards have received national recognition for successful design and implementation.

The governor's nine-member Advisory Board of Arthritis developed the first statewide self-help arthritis course. This course, which is designed to help individuals improve the quality of their lives through daily management of arthritis, is a model for other state programs. Other activities of this board include encouraging professional education for community health workers and physicians and recommendations for projects in lupus and arthritis research.

The Diabetes Task Force, a thirteen-member lay and professional advisory board, initiated a coordinated plan to increase patient competency in self-care and in coping with diabetes. This program also enhances provider proficiency in caring for diabetics. The Pennsylvania Diabetes Academy, the only such organization of its kind in the nation, provides professional education for physicians, nurses, and other persons who assist diabetic patients.

For further information on topics in this chapter, see the following sources in *Key to Further Information:*

Pennsylvania Medical Society

Also see the Blue Pages of your telephone directory

11

Human Services

Pennsylvania provides an array of family and individual support services designed to reduce or eliminate dependency and to improve the quality of life for the state's most vulnerable citizens. Job training and employment services, care for disadvantaged children and older citizens, and comprehensive mental-health programs are available to this population. The departments of Welfare, Agriculture, Aging, Education, Health, Labor and Industry, and Commerce participate in providing these services.

Pennsylvania ranks third in the nation in medical expenditures for the poor and spends more per senior citizen on programs specifically for the elderly than any other state.

Department of Public Welfare

Through its programs for low-income, poor, and unemployed persons, children, and youth, the visually handicapped, and mentally disabled, the Department of Public Welfare (DPW) serves close to two million Pennsylvanians. DPW assists persons in becoming financially independent, provides community living arrangements for those unable to care for themselves due to mental or physical disability, and delivers hospital care when alternatives are not appropriate.

The Public Welfare Code of 1967 directs the Department of Public Welfare to

> promote the welfare and happiness of all of the people of the Commonwealth, by providing public assistance to all of its needy and distressed; that assistance shall be administered promptly and humanely with due regard for the preservation of family life . . .
> and in such a way and manner as to encourage self-respect, self-dependency and the desire to be a good citizen and useful to society.

Administration of the Department of Public Welfare

The Secretary of Public Welfare is appointed by the governor and confirmed by the Senate. Each secretary organizes the department to reflect program objectives. Usually an executive deputy secretary is appointed to oversee a number of deputy secretaries. In 1988 the department's deputy secretaries were responsible for the following: administration; policy, planning, and evaluation; fraud and abuse investigation and recovery; income maintenance; medical-assistance; children, youth, and families; mental health; and mental retardation.

Program planning, policy determination, and budgeting are administered by the department's central office in Harrisburg. Four regional offices direct the operation of institutions and county

Basic Human Needs in Pennsylvania

Areas of Need	Individuals
Aid to Families with Dependent Children	542,612
(1987 Dept. of Public Welfare data)	
General Assistance (DPW)	154,655
Supplemental Security Income (DPW)	179,322
Medical Assistance (DPW)	1,191,570
Food Stamps (DPW)	975,902
WIC: Supplemental food service program for	179,155
women, infants, and children	
State Food Purchase Program, Dept. of Agr.	2,310,271
(incomplete reporting) 1986–87	
Economically Disadvantaged*	2,209,900
(A member of a family who receives cash assistance or	
whose family income does not exceed the poverty level	
or 70% of the lower living standard income level)	
Dislocated Workers*	116,500
(A person who has been or will soon be terminated or	
laid off from employment and is unlikely to return to	
previous industry)	
1986 annual average	
Persons 16–64 with a work disability	642,761
1980 census*	
High School Dropouts (1985–86 school year)*	23,324
Teenage Mothers (1986)*	35,412
Displaced Homemakers (1985)*	313,000
Female Single Parents (1980 census)	219,907
Average monthly number of persons receiving	749,888
cash welfare assistance (1986)*	
Long-Term Unemployment (15+ weeks) (1986)*	120,000
Population of Pennsylvania, 1985 estimate	**11,853,400**

Annual Planning Information Report, Pennsylvania Office of Employment Security, 1987.

assistance offices. They also supervise and monitor all programs and services funded by the department.

The Department of Public Welfare operates sixty-seven county assistance offices, six offices for the visually handicapped, and the following institutions: fourteen mental hospitals and one restoration center; ten centers for the mentally retarded, five youth institutions, two restoration centers for the elderly and six general hospitals. The department employs more than 11,000 persons.

As a combined city/county government, Philadelphia is the only municipality in the state that actually operates a welfare department. The departmental budget is administered by a commissioner who reports to the mayor.

The Family Assistance Management Information System (FAMIS), a computerized database, gives DPW caseworkers access to information on client participation in the cash assistance, medical-assistance, food stamp, low-income energy assistance grant, and work registration programs.

No person in the Commonwealth may be excluded, overtly or covertly, from participating in any program or activity of DPW on the basis of race, color, sex, creed, national origin, age, sexual preference, or handicap. The nondiscrimination policy applies equally to department employees, to clients, and to agencies who contract with the department for client services.

Budget

DPW operates one of the largest programs in the country and receives the largest appropriation of any Pennsylvania agency. The budget for 1987–88 totaled over $5.75 billion. Federal funds allocated under Title XX of the Social Security Act (known as the social services block grant) account for 43 percent of the budget.

Title XX funds provide the basic support for income maintenance, children, youth, and families, mental-health, and mental-retardation programs. Services are delivered through thirteen broad program areas and assist more than 900,000 persons.

The Office of Income Maintenance in the Department of Public Welfare administers the public-assistance program, and employees in county offices determine eligibility. Programs include the following: Aid to Families with Dependent Children, funded half and half by federal and state funds; General Assistance, totally state funded; Supplemental Security Income, federal and state funds; the federal Food Stamp Program; and the State Blind Pension program. Once the county assistance staff determines that a person is eligible for cash assistance, that person is automatically eligible for medical assistance. Eligibility is determined by the federal poverty level.

Family Assistance Programs

In 1987 the average number of nondisabled persons who received a monthly general assistance cash grant was 677,000. The payment to a family of four ranged from $433 to $490 depending on the part of the state in which the family lived.

Supplemental Security Income (SSI), a federal program administered through the Social Security Administration, provides cash assistance for the elderly or for people of any age who are blind or disabled. Pennsylvania adds a cash supplement to the federal payment. Persons receiving SSI are also eligible for medical-assistance benefits and social services through the county assistance offices.

A special SSI supplement is available to disabled persons residing in state-certified personal care and nursing homes. This program is designed to provide individuals with an alternative to hospitalization.

Employment of Cash Assistance Recipients

All cash-assistance recipients are required to register for work placement or special training programs. Persons who are unemployed and able-bodied, but who have not located work, must participate in the Employment and Training Program (ETP). The ETP has three components: the New Directions program provides help to identify barriers to employment and provides referral to appropriate social-service providers; the Community Work Experience Program provides meaningful work experience for assistance recipients; and the Office of Employment Security obtains employment for those who are classified as job-ready.

The Employment Incentive Payment Program (EIPP) provides federal and state tax credits to businesses for up to three years, to employ a cash-assistance recipient for at least one year.

The Single Point of Contact (SPOC) is a demonstration program sponsored by the departments of Labor and Industry, Welfare, and Education. The program, designed to help persons become self-supporting, provides education and training, job placement, and case-management services to those on public assistance through a single application process.

The Bureau of Blindness and Visual Services offers a variety of services for the visually handicapped and blind through six district offices. It provides business opportunities within state government by franchising snack bars and vending facilities to visually-impaired entrepreneurs. The office also handles counseling, rehabilitation, and social service programs for the visually handicapped funded through Title XX of the Social Security Act.

Pennsylvania provides a pension for the blind, totally state funded, available to those persons who meet state requirements but who are not eligible for Supplemental Security Income.

Services for the Visually Handicapped

The medical-assistance program is a federal-state program (funded approximately fifty-fifty) that provides quality health care for more than one million low-income Pennsylvania residents. The program pays for inpatient hospital care, outpatient clinic care, laboratory work, and X-ray fees in private and public facilities for mentally or physically disabled who are eligible, and nursing-home care for those who have exhausted their financial resources. Physician, chiropractic, dental, optometric, podiatric care, and drug and alcohol therapy services are also funded through medical-assistance. These funds supplement the federal medicare program.

Persons on public assistance or those who receive Supplemental Security Income payments are automatically eligible for medical-assistance benefits. Other low-income individuals and families may be eligible if they meet certain income limitations. Medical-assistance may supplement an individual's health insurance or other benefits.

Medical Assistance

The medical-assistance Transportation Program provides funds to county governments for transportation for public-assistance clients to receive medical services.

Food Programs

The Food Stamp Program, a U.S. Department of Agriculture program, is administered through the county assistance offices. The program is federally funded, except for the administrative costs, which are shared by the state.

To be eligible for food stamps, a person must meet certain income limitations, have the facilities to prepare home-cooked meals, and be the head of a household. In addition to grocery store purchases, food stamps can be used for home-delivered meals and for the purchase of seeds and plants. Stamps are made available in emergency situations to victims of natural disasters. The amount of food stamps to which a person is entitled depends on the monthly income and the size of the household. Income limits are revised every six months by the U.S. Department of Agriculture to keep pace with the cost of living. An applicant cannot be denied food stamps for the lack of a fixed address.

The Pennsylvania Department of Agriculture administers the federal surplus food program and supplements that program with cash grants to counties to purchase food for the needy. Grants are awarded on the basis of the numbers of persons in emergency need; counties select nonprofit organizations to distribute the food. This program brings needy persons who would not ordinarily seek help into the human service system and provides them access to the rest of system services.

Through a network of contracted private providers, Pennsylvania supports protective services to persons in actual or threatened abuse situations. Emergency shelter and medical, counseling, preventive, and advocacy services are furnished to those who are victims of assault, rape, or domestic violence.

In 1988 special legislation established the elder abuse intervention program, which provides protective services to persons over the age of sixty.

The Department of Pubic Welfare has a twenty-four-hour toll-free hotline for reporting suspected cases of child abuse and serious neglect. The Child Protective Act of 1975 requires physicians, teachers, school personnel, and other professionals who come in daily contact with children to report suspected cases of abuse. The public can also report suspected abuse. Reports are investigated through the child protective services unit of the county child-welfare agency and appropriate action is taken to protect any abused child.

Victims who have sustained a financial loss or injury due to a criminal act are eligible for compensation through the Crime Victims Compensation Board. An innocent crime victim can be reimbursed for medical or related expenses, counseling, funeral expenses, loss of earnings, or loss of cash benefits. The maximum award is $35,000.

Protective Services and Victim Compensation

The Office for Children, Youth, and Families provides both child-welfare services and state facilities for delinquent children. Welfare services to families include adoption, counseling, family planning, life-skills education, and homemaker services. Foster family care, group homes, short-term

Services to Children and Youth

institutional care, and protection against abuse are available to children. These programs are carried out through the sixty-seven county child-welfare agencies under contract with the Department of Public Welfare. County commissioners must designate an individual or a single agency to develop an annual plan to improve coordination of child welfare and youth services. The plan must include all expenditures for both child-welfare agencies and juvenile court services.

County agencies are reimbursed by the state for part of the child-welfare program and administrative costs; the percentage varies with each program. The state reimburses 50 percent of the cost of actual care and support of juveniles committed to an institution by a county child welfare agency or by the courts.

Child Development (Day Care)

The purpose of Pennsylvania's subsidized child-care program is to facilitate the parents' or caretakers' ability to work or participate in work training by providing their children with a safe and stimulating environment. Day-care services are provided on a sliding-fee scale to children from birth to twelve years of age from families with low-income who demonstrate this need. Since publicly funded day care was introduced in 1968, the number of children in the program has risen from 5,000 to almost 25,000 in 1988. The Department of Public Welfare contracts with a variety of agencies for day-care services under Title XX of the Social Security Act and state funds. The day-care appropriation is over 29 percent of DPW's Title XX funds. State funds supplement day-care services.

Specialists in DPW's four regional offices supervise and monitor day-care programs and inspect and license both private and public day-care centers. The welfare code sets minimum standards for child-care programs, including construction of the centers, equipment, operation, and services provided. In addition, federal interagency day-care regulations apply to programs funded totally or in part from federal funds.

All personnel working in day-care centers are required to have a background check conducted by the state police. Act 33 of 1986 prohibits persons with a criminal record from working in day-care centers, and provides for screening to indicate whether an applicant's record includes incidents involving child abuse.

Youth Institutions

The Department of Public Welfare operates three youth developmental centers, two youth forestry camps, and three secure facilities for the care and treatment of delinquent youths. The department provides funds for police units assigned to juvenile cases, for programs designed to prevent delinquency, and for systems to increase planning and coordination of youth services.

Children who have committed status offenses (truancy and other noncriminal acts) are categorized as dependent and treatment must be provided in appropriate facilities. Act 41 of 1976 prohibits declaring any child under ten delinquent, or the commitment of any child under twelve to a state institution, or the housing of juveniles in county jails. The department's programs for young people are designed to provide care and treatment, whenever possible, in small community-based treatment programs; only when absolutely necessary are they placed in secure institutions.

The department's regional offices regulate and inspect privately operated facilities such as youth treatment centers.

Mental Health and Mental Retardation Services

Care for the mentally ill and mentally retarded in Pennsylvania is focused on treatment in the community so that persons receive the services they need while remaining in their home environment. Eighty-nine community centers provide information and referral, short-term inpatient, partial hospitalization, outpatient, social and vocational rehabilitation, and services to persons who have been discharged from hospital or residential programs. In addition, they collect demographic and client problem information that can be used by other agencies. Ninety percent of the funding comes from federal and state sources and client fees. The county in which the center operates funds 10 percent of the program.

Community programs provide services to preschool and adult mentally retarded citizens. The local education system provides mental retardation services for all school-age clients (See chapter 9, Education.)

The Mental Health Procedure Act of 1976 gives mentally ill people the right to receive treatment in the least restrictive setting possible. It mandates that involuntary emergency examination and commitment are possible only when persons present a clear and present danger to harm themselves or others. The law requires that all involuntarily committed patients be evaluated periodically to assess the need for continued hospital treatment.

Pennsylvania supports fifteen state mental hospitals, one restoration center for the mentally ill, and nine state centers for the mentally retarded. DPW policy continues to emphasize community living arrangements for mentally disabled persons and during the last two decades has aggressively expanded community living arrangements. The number of patients in state mental hospitals has declined from 33,000 in 1966 to under 8,000 in 1987. The number of residents at the state centers for the mentally retarded has also declined. In 1987 almost 7,200 mentally retarded persons, almost half of them former residents of state institutions, lived in group homes, apartments, or other community residential settings. Each client receives a state stipend for housing and food costs.

Low-Income Home Energy Assistance Program

The federally funded Low-Income Home Energy Assistance Program (LIHEAP) provides financial assistance to families least able to afford to heat their homes. Cash payments are made to fuel distributors and utility companies on behalf of eligible families, or directly to those households whose home heating costs are included in their rent. Emergency payments are available to repair heating equipment, to provide fuel, or to restore service to customers with delinquent accounts. The program is funded through a federal block grant and administered by the Department of Welfare. Fifteen percent of the block grant goes to weatherization programs administered by the Department of Community Affairs for homes of low-income persons.

Department of Aging

One of only a few such cabinet-level agencies in the nation, the Department of Aging, established in 1978, serves as an advocate for the concerns of older persons. The department programs deal with nutrition education, employment, transportation, in-home care and protection, long-term care assessment, and management services for seniors.

Advocacy brings the special needs of the elderly to the attention of state agencies. The Bureau of Advocacy offers seniors legal, income maintenance, health, and community services. The department administers the Prescription Assistance Program, which subsidizes prescription costs (see chapter 10, Public Health) and prepares the federally mandated State Plan on Aging.

Area Agencies on Aging

Fifty-one Area Agencies on Aging (AAA) offer casework, reassurance, homemaker services, transportation, information and referral, adult day care, and friendly visitor services. Senior citizen centers are operated by thirteen private nonprofit corporations and thirty-eight county agencies. These centers usually provide meals as well as a variety of socialization, recreational, and educational activities. All persons aged sixty and over are eligible for AAA services.

Other Human Service Support Programs

- The Office of Vocational Rehabilitation in the Department of Labor and Industry provides a wide range of services designed to rehabilitate handicapped individuals so that they can obtain gainful employment.
- Unemployment Compensation is an insurance program administered through the Department of Labor and Industry providing for temporary replacement of a portion of wages lost due to unemployment that is not the fault of the worker.

- The Department of Education operates special programs to assist displaced workers to find gainful employment and to become economically self-sufficient.
- Mentally alert but severely physically disabled persons can apply for federally funded attendant-care services to enable them to live as independently as possible in their own homes. Payments are based on monthly gross income.
- The homeless can receive food stamps and are eligible to receive funds to assist with rent or security deposits. Counties provide emergency shelter for those in immediate need of housing.
- The state provides legal services at no cost for low-income persons involved in civil legal actions through the Pennsylvania Legal Services Corporation.

Citizen Participation

Citizen participation is essential in defining service needs and developing programs to address these needs. A number of advisory and administrative boards and committees afford citizens the opportunity to participate in decisions and programs related to public assistance and human services. Members serve without pay but are reimbursed for travel and other expenses incurred in the performance of their duties.

Each of the sixty-seven counties in Pennsylvania has a county board of assistance composed of up to fifteen members appointed by the governor and confirmed by the Senate. These administrative boards are responsible for hiring county welfare employees.

The medical-assistance Advisory Committee, the Income Maintenance Advisory Committee, low-income Home Energy Assistance Program Advisory Committee, and the Employment and Training Advisory Committee all provide direction to bureaus within the Department of Welfare.

The Pennsylvania Consumer Provider Council on Blindness, the State Deaf-Blind Advisory Committee, and the Elected Committee of Blind Vendors for the Business Enterprises Program advise DPW on provision of service to these special populations.

A nine-member Advisory Committee for Mental Health and Mental Retardation (MH/MR), appointed by the governor, provides advice on client eligibility, service standards, and licensure of agencies and institutions. Thirteen-member boards, one in each county, advise county MH/MR administrators on matters affecting the provision of mental health and mental-retardation services.

Each state mental hospital and state mental retardation center has a nine-member board of trustees to advise the hospital superintendent/administrator on program policy and management. Full-time advocates contracted through United Mental Health, Inc., provide ombudsman services to hospital patients.

The Pennsylvania Council on Aging, a nineteen-member council appointed by the governor, assists the Secretary of Aging to promote programs to maximize independence and involvement of older Pennsylvanians. It also evaluates program and department operations and prepares the State Plan on Aging.

Each department involved in the provision of human services provides an opportunity for citizens to make recommendations on social service programs through public hearings at the local, regional, and state levels.

For further information, check specific topics in the Blue Pages of your telephone directory.

12

Natural Resources

P ublic attitudes toward the natural environment have changed dramatically in the past twenty-five years. Recognition that natural resources are finite and that they are vital to survival has led to passage of legislation to improve their management and protection.

The Commonwealth became constitutionally responsible for the protection of the environment and the conservation of natural resources in 1971, when voters approved an addition to the Declaration of Rights of the constitution.

> The people have a right to clean air, pure water, and to the preservation of the natural, scenic, historic and esthetic values of the environment. Pennsylvania's public natural resources are the common property of all the people, including generations yet to come. As trustee of these resources, the Commonwealth shall conserve and maintain them for the benefit of all the people. (Article 1, Sec. 27)

The primary responsibility for natural-resource management and environmental protection lies with the Department of Environmental Resources. Other agencies with responsibilities for natural resources include the Fish and Game Commissions, the Pennsylvania Energy Office, and the departments of Agriculture and Community Affairs.

Department of Environmental Resources

The Department of Environmental Resources (DER), created by Act 275 of 1970, is charged with the responsibility for ensuring the wise use of Pennsylvania's natural resources and protecting and restoring the natural environment. The department develops plans and enforces regulations on air quality, water quality, liquid and solid waste management, safe drinking water, mining and mine safety, oil and gas drilling, dam safety, and wetlands protection. It is the custodian for the state forests and state parks and is responsible for the management of water resources.

Administration

Because the air and bodies of water do not recognize political or geographic boundaries, cooperation among various levels of government is vital to ensure clean air and water. The department coordinates activities and provides technical assistance on air quality, water supplies, sewage disposal, and solid waste management.

The two major areas of the department's work are carried out by the Deputy Secretary for Environmental Protection and the Deputy Secretary for Resources Management. Support services for the department are provided by the Deputy Secretary for Administration and the Deputy Secretary for Public Liaison. The public may contact this secretary with specific questions on environmental issues.

Six regional environmental protection offices, located in Harrisburg, Meadville, Pittsburgh, Norristown, Wilkes-Barre, and Williamsport, enforce environmental laws in their respective regions. The litigation offices in Harrisburg, Pittsburgh, and Philadelphia initiate all enforcement actions, defend appeals from department actions, and supervise department personnel when conducting investigations and tests for use in enforcement actions. These three field offices provide counsel to the regional offices of the department on daily enforcement, inspection, and policy problems to assure statewide uniformity.

Budget

DER operated on a budget of approximately $286 million in 1986–87, more than a quarter of which was in federal funds. Projected expenditures for 1988–89 total $396 million. The largest category of expenditure is for environmental management and protection.

The major state laws affecting the protection of the environment are the Clean Streams Law, the Air Pollution Control Act, the Solid Waste Management Act, the Sewage Facilities Act, the Radiation Protection Act, the Surface Mine Conservation and Reclamation Act, and the Oil and Gas Act.

Environmental Protection

Air-Quality Control

The cost of air pollution to society is high. It may affect the health of citizens, destroy vegetation, and lower environmental quality. The cost of controlling air pollution is also high, often requiring heavy investments in research and equipment. The federal Clean Air Act gives states and local governments the primary responsibility for air pollution planning and enforcement.

The Bureau of Air Quality Control develops and implements programs for control of air pollution within the state, assuring compliance with the state Air Pollution Control Act and the federal Clean Air Act through monitoring, education, and enforcement. The bureau investigates complaints and initiates remedial action to abate air-pollutant sources, establishes procedures to advise affected areas, provides guidance to industry and citizen groups, and works with other state, local, and federal agencies to establish effective clean-air programs.

Three areas of the state (Philadelphia, Pittsburgh, and the Allentown-Bethlehem-Easton area) that do not meet federal air-quality standards for ozone have additional air-pollution-control programs, including automobile emissions inspections and maintenance (I&M). The I&M program is administered by the Bureau of Motor Vehicles in the Department of Transportation.

Water-Quality Control

Clean water is both an essential element of a healthful environment and a most valuable resource. Various government agencies are engaged in managing and protecting water supplies.

The Bureau of Water Quality Management is responsible for developing and monitoring water-quality standards for both surface and ground-water and for regulating sewage treatment plants. It enforces the state's Clean Streams Law and the Sewage Facilities Act and cooperates with the Environmental Protection Agency under the federal Water Quality Act.

The bureau administers federal and state grants for construction of public sewage systems and the permit programs that regulate discharges from public and private sewage and industrial waste treatment plants into the waters of the state. The bureau provides oversight and technical assistance to municipalities in carrying out their planning, permitting, and enforcement responsibilities for sewage disposal under the Sewage Facilities Act. Training and certification are provided for local sewage enforcement officers and sewage treatment plant operators.

Control of sedimentation pollution of waterways is the responsibility of the Bureau of Soil and Water Conservation, which administers planning and permitting programs for earth-moving activities. Much of this program is delegated to county conservation districts, and the state provides them with some funding assistance.

The Safe Drinking Water Act, which regulates public water supplies, is administered by the Bureau of Community Environmental Control. Twenty-eight district and regional offices are also responsible for monitoring food protection in public eating and drinking places and environmental sanitation at public facilities, such as campgrounds, public bathing areas, and schools.

The unsolved problem of acid mine drainage from abandoned mines is the single largest cause of stream degradation in the state and continues to trouble those responsible for water quality protection. Although new mines are no longer permitted to discharge acid drainage into streams, the cost of correcting the existing problem is estimated to be $3–5 billion.

In 1988 voters approved a $300 million bond issue for repair and construction of water supply and sewage treatment systems essential for protecting public health and promoting economic development. This long-term public works program, called Pennvest, is administered by the Pennsylvania Infrastructure Investment Authority with the assistance of the Bureaus of Water Quality Management and Community Environmental Control.

Waste Management and Hazardous Materials

Solid-waste management remains a pressing problem facing Pennsylvanians. Annually 7.3 million tons of solid waste are generated in the state, including household, commercial, and industrial waste, hazardous waste, and sewage sludge. Many of these wastes are improperly handled and can cause air, water, land-use, and health-related problems. Landfill areas are becoming scarce. Many private and municipal collection systems are inadequate and fail to meet minimum standards.

In 1988 the responsibility for municipal waste-management and waste-disposal planning was transferred from municipalities to the sixty-seven counties with the goal of finding more efficient regional solutions. At the same time mandatory recycling of selected materials such as glass, aluminum cans, newspapers, and high-grade office paper became law, to go into effect for two-thirds of the state's residents by 1991–92. From a list of recyclable materials listed in the law, municipalities may select three for recycling in their area.

The Bureau of Waste Management is responsible for statewide planning, permitting, inspection, investigation, and enforcement of waste-management facilities under the state Solid Waste Management Act and related federal laws, including the Resource Conservation and Recovery Act and the Comprehensive Environmental Resources Compensation and Liability Act (Superfund). The bureau administers grant programs for solid-waste-management planning and recycling, and resource recovery projects.

Programs for hazardous and industrial waste planning and regulation and abandoned site investigation and cleanup are also administered by the bureau. More than two thousand sites containing hazardous materials have been identified in the state and cleanup is a major problem. Planned spending for this in 1988 represents nearly a four-fold increase over funds spent the previous year, reflecting heightened concern over this danger to citizens' well-being. A state fund based on the Capital Stock and Franchise Tax was created in 1987 to supplement federal Superfund monies.

The Bureau of Radiation Protection is responsible for overseeing development of a site by a private contractor for a low-level radioactive waste disposal facility that will serve the states in the Appalachian Low Level Radioactive Waste Compact: Delaware, Maryland, West Virginia, and Pennsylvania.

The bureau also conducts an environmental radiation-monitoring program, nuclear safety review, and cooperates with the federal Nuclear Regulatory Commission on oversight of nuclear power plants and emergency radiation response programs. Education and technical assistance on radon-monitoring detection and remediation programs are provided by the bureau, as well as a licensing program for contractors involved with radon activities.

Mining, Oil, and Gas

Three bureaus share the responsibility for enforcing state mining laws and reclaiming abandoned mine sites. The Bureau of Deep Mine Safety provides for the health and safety of workers in and around underground mines. The Bureau of Mining and Reclamation administers a permitting, inspection, and enforcement program for all mining and land-reclamation activities, mine subsidence regulation, and coal refuse disposal. It also administers the mine subsidence insurance program. The Bureau of Abandoned Mine Reclamation maintains an index of abandoned mine sites and administers programs for restoration of abandoned sites using funds generated from forfeited bonds, reclamation fees, and the federal Abandoned Mine Lands Program. Total cost to reclaim all abandoned mine sites in Pennsylvania is estimated to be $13–15 billion.

The Bureau of Oil and Gas Management is responsible for statewide oil and gas regulatory programs, including oil- and gas-well operations, plugging of abandoned wells, underground natural-gas storage, and waste-disposal activities associated with drilling.

Resources Management

DER administers programs and manages state owned lands to protect and restore the natural environment, to protect public health and safety, to provide opportunities for outdoor recreation, and to enhance the quality of life for all Pennsylvanians.

The Deputate for Resource Management includes the Bureaus of Water Resources Management, Dams and Waterway Management, and Topographic and Geologic Survey.

Responsibility for various water-resource programs lies with the Bureau of Water Resource Management. The bureau has developed a state water plan that describes water-resource problems and needs and recommends alternatives for increasing water supply. The bureau sponsors water-conservation education and technical assistance programs. Water allocation permits for public water suppliers withdrawing water from surface sources are issued by the bureau. The Division of Scenic Rivers administers the law that sets up a process for identifying state wild and scenic rivers and develops programs to protect them. The Division of Coastal Zone Management, in cooperation with federal and local governments, reviews activities in Pennsylvania's coastal zones along the Delaware estuary and Lake Erie to ensure their conformity with federal and state coastal-zone-protection laws. The division provides some funding for local projects such as waterfront plans and recreation access to the waterfront.

The Bureau of Dams and Waterways Management administers the Dam Safety and Encroachments Act, which regulates encroachments in lakes, streams, and wetlands of Pennsylvania. The bureau cooperates with the U.S. Army Corps of Engineers in this regulatory program. A wetlands protection policy to promote cooperation between federal and state agencies is currently being developed. The bureau is also responsible for administering the storm-water-management program and provides grants to counties for storm-water-management planning. Licensing of hydroelectric facilities is another bureau activity.

The Bureau of Topographic and Geologic Survey plans, administers, and conducts comprehensive and detailed surveys of the geology, mineral resources, topography, and ground-water resources of the state and makes the results available to the public through publications, technical services, and a geologic library.

Parks and Forests

Millions of residents and visitors annually use the state parks with their year-round recreation facilities for picnicking, boating, swimming, hiking, hunting, and winter sports. No fees are charged for admission to state parks, but some activities such as camping and pool swimming do require a fee. Every resident is within twenty-five miles of a state park.

The Bureau of State Parks has responsibility for supervision, maintenance, planning, development, regulation, and preservation of state parks for the purpose of promoting healthful outdoor recreation. The state park system offers a wide variety of recreational opportunities in 113 state parks and environmental education centers. More than 280,000 acres are included in the state park system.

Sixty historic sites and museums, including five historical parks, are administered by the Pennsylvania Historical and Museum Commission.

Forests cover 65 percent of Pennsylvania's land, providing recreation for citizens and protection for watersheds and wildlife. The state owns and administers more than two million acres of forest land.

The Bureau of Forestry, through its twenty district offices, manages state forest lands for multiple-use purposes, including recreation, timbering, and wildlife and watershed protection. The bureau is responsible for the protection of state forests from forest fire, insects, and disease. Funds from timber sales are used to augment funding for operation of the bureau, with some of the money going directly to the state general fund.

Independent Agencies

The Fish Commission enforces regulations relating to boating and to the protection, propagation, distribution, and catching of fish. It manages hatching stations, conducts research, and enforces watercraft safety. It is financed primarily by the sale of fishing and boating licenses and some federal funds.

The Pennsylvania Energy Office, an independent state agency that reports to the lieutenant governor, is responsible for promoting the development of the state's indigenous energy resources. Strong emphasis is placed on promoting energy efficiency and conservation and coordinating federal energy grants.

The Game Commission is responsible for the protection, propagation, and preservation of game, fur-bearing animals, and protected birds; for the training of game protectors, who enforce game laws and promote wildlife conservation; and for managing 1.2 million acres of state game lands. It is financed by the sale of hunting licenses (more than one million are sold annually) and by revenue from mineral, oil, and gas leases on game lands.

The Environmental Hearing Board (EHB) is a

quasi-judicial arm of DER that holds hearings and issues opinions, orders, and adjudications upon appeals from action taken by the department.

Department of Agriculture

Two natural-resource-related programs can be found in the Department of Agriculture. The Bureau of Agricultural Development is responsible for farmland preservation programs and administration of the various laws designed to keep farmland in agricultural use. These include the Clean and Green Act, which provides for a lower property tax on lands that are in agricultural or forestry use, and the Agricultural Area Security Act, which provides benefits to farmers who agree to establish agricultural security areas where farming is the predominant use. In 1987 voters approved a $100 million bond issue to fund the purchase of development rights in these areas.

Conservation Districts

Sixty-six county conservation districts perform local conservation-related activities. Established under the Conservation District Law and funded jointly by the state and the county, conservation districts cooperate with federal and state conservation agencies and assist DER in the enforcement of sedimentation control regulations.

Basin Commissions

Pennsylvania is part of two river-basin commissions that are unique in that the member states and the federal government have equal voices in their operation. The Delaware River Basin Commission and the Susquehanna River Basin Commission are organized under individual compacts that have been approved by Congress. These two commissions have planning powers to provide for the management of basin water and related land resources, as well as specific regulatory powers enumerated in the individual compacts.

The Commonwealth also participates in several interstate river-basin commissions with advisory powers only. These include the Interstate Commission on the Potomac River Basin, the Ohio River Basin Commission, the Great Lakes Commission, and the Chesapeake Bay Commission.

Citizen Participation

Citizens Advisory Council (CAC) to DER reviews all environmental laws of the Commonwealth and makes appropriate suggestions for their revision and modification. It also reviews the work of DER, makes recommendations for improvements, and reports annually to the governor and the General Assembly.

The CAC periodically conducts hearings throughout the state on citizens' environmental concerns. The nineteen-member council includes the Secretary of Environmental Resources. The governor, the president pro tempore of the Senate, and the speaker of the House each appoint six members. No more than three of each group of appointments may be of the same political party.

The Environmental Quality Board, composed of secretaries of various executive departments and including five members of the CAC and four members of the legislature, formulates and adopts rules and regulations for the performance of DER.

Numerous citizen groups in the state monitor current events relating to conservation matters and testify on legislative and regulatory issues concerning the environment. Communications among these groups are enhanced by a Conservation Network. DER has organized citizen roundtables at the state and regional levels to promote information exchange between the department and the public.

For further information on topics in this chapter, see the following sources in *Key to Further Information:*

Department of Environmental Resources, Office of Public Liaison

League of Women Voters of Pennsylvania

Key to Further Information

Basic sources of information about Pennsylvania government that were used in the preparation of this book are listed below. Because government is constantly changing, no printed compilation of facts can be continuously up to date. Current information can be obtained from governmental departments and agencies, from elected officials, and from civic organizations.

Sources for General Information on State Government

Administrative Code of Pennsylvania. These volumes, organized by executive department, contain administrative laws for the operation of Pennsylvania government. Code is available in regional library centers and some local libraries, or from Administrator of Pennsylvania Courts, 1414 Three Penn Center Plaza, Philadelphia, PA 19102.

A Citizen's Guide to Pennsylvania Local Government, Bureau of Local Government Services, Department of Community Affairs (DCA), Commonwealth of Pennsylvania. A comprehensive discussion of the structure and functions of local governmental units. Available from DCA.

All About Elections in Pennsylvania, Department of State, Commonwealth of Pennsylvania. A guide to the electoral process in Pennsylvania, including sections on voter registration, nomination of candidates, and voting. Available from your local legislator.

Commonwealth of Pennsylvania Executive Budget. Full budget and executive summary are published prior to budget presentation. The document contains budget rationale as well as line-item expenditures. Full text available in local libraries. Summaries are available from governor's office.

Commonwealth of Pennsylvania Legislative Journal. The Journal is published each day that the General Assembly is in session, with the House and Senate proceedings in separate sections. It is the official record of legislative proceedings. Available from the office of the secretary of the Senate, the chief clerk of the House, or from your state senator or representative.

Commonwealth Telephone Directory. Directory gives addresses and telephone numbers of elected and staff persons working in Harrisburg. Available for use in local state senator or representative offices and can be purchased at the State Book Store.

Constitution of the Commonwealth of Pennsylvania. Available at most libraries, also reprinted in *The Pennsylvania Manual.*

Department of Environmental Resources, Office of Public Liaison, 9th Floor Fulton Building, Third and Locust Streets, P.O. Box 2063, Harrisburg, PA 17120, 717–787–1323.

Legislative Reference Bureau, 641 Main Capitol Building, P.O. Box 1127, Harrisburg, PA 17120, 717–787–2342. Bureau provides information on the status of bills.

League of Women Voters of Pennsylvania Information Center, P.O. Box 607, Harrisburg, PA 17108–0607, 1–800–692–7281. This office can provide you with information on legislative action, voting information, League publications, and direct you to local League services.

Pennsylvania Bar Association, 100 South Street, P.O. Box 186, Harrisburg, PA 17108, 1–800–932–0311.

Pennsylvania Chamber of Business and Industry, 222 North Third Street, Harrisburg, PA 17101, 717–255–3252. The State Chamber is the state's largest business organization. It provides information on business climate and public/private business development programs, and monitors legislation affecting business.

Pennsylvania Economy League, Inc. 105 North Front Street, Harrisburg, PA 17108, 717–234–3151. The League undertakes comprehensive studies of state and local government.

Pennsylvania Legislative Directory. The directory, printed during each two-year legislative session, contains information about legislators' districts, committee assignments, and office locations. Available from the Chief Clerk and through your local legislator.

Pennsylvania Federation of Teachers, 1816 Chestnut Street, Philadelphia, PA 19103, 215–587–

6738. The PFT has available information concerning legislative issues affecting teachers and general information on school operations.

Pennsylvania Medical Society, 20 Eford Road, P.O. Box 602, Lemoyne, PA 17043–0602, 1–800–228–7823.

Pennsylvania School Boards Association, Inc., 774 Limekiln Road, New Cumberland, PA 17070, 717–774–2331. The PSBA has general information concerning public school finance and operation. Publishes a variety of publications for school board members and the public.

Pennsylvania School Code. A compilation of the school laws of Pennsylvania. Code is available in regional library centers and some local libraries.

Pennsylvania State Education Association, 400 North Third Street, P.O. Box 1724, Harrisburg, PA 17105, 717–255–7000. The PSEA has available information concerning legislative issues affecting teachers and general information on school operations.

Pennsylvania Statistical Abstracts, Bureau of Statistics, Department of Commerce. A compilation of statistics that provides information on such topics as population, housing, education, commerce, social services, and state and local taxes. Available from the State Book Store.

Purdon's Pennsylvania Statutes, annotated. A compilation of general and permanent laws from 1700 to the present, with annual updates. Available at most libraries.

"The Pennsylvania Legislative Process." This pamphlet, prepared for distribution by local legislators, describes the legislative process and the legislative committee system, and has a section on parliamentary procedure. It is also available from the Chief Clerk of the House, State Capitol, Harrisburg, PA 17120.

The Pennsylvania Manual, Department of General Services, Commonwealth of Pennsylvania, editor Ozzie Doukas. Manual contains the Pennsylvania Constitution, a history of the state, biographies of General Assembly members and description of executive departments and the judiciary, and lists state governmental bodies and other factual information.

State Book Store, Department of General Services, Tenth and Market Streets, P.O. Box 1365, Harrisburg, PA 17105, 717–787–5109. The bookstore has manuals, state statistical information, special reports relating to government operation, and maps available for sale to the public.

Toll-Free Telephone Numbers

Child Abuse Hotline   1–800–932–0313
Consumer Protection (PA)   1–800–441–2555
Day Care Eligibility Line   1–800–222–2149
Drug and Alcohol Abuse   1–800–932–0912
Energy Assistance (Department of Public Welfare)
    1–800–692–7462
Food Stamps (Department of Public Welfare)   1–800–692–7462
Governor's Action Center   1–800–932–0784
Health Information   1–800–692–7254
League of Women Voters Legislative Information Center
    1–800–692–7281
Motor Vehicle Information   1–800–932–4600
Pennsylvania Higher Education Assistance Agency (PHEAA)
    1–800–692–7392
Pennsylvania Protection and Advocacy   1–800–692–7443
Prescription Drug Assistance for Seniors   1–800–225–7223
Property Tax/Rent Rebate Claims   1–800–772–5246
Public Utility Commission   1–800–692–7380
Welfare, General Assistance   1–800–692–7462
Worker's Compensation   1–800–482–2383

Index